TEENYAGE RUNAWAY

MEMOIRS OF A 1960S HIPPY

RONALD SCHULZ

Tumbleweed Books

Tumble through the pages of our books

TEENAGE RUNAWAY
RONALD J SCHULZ

Tumbleweed Books
Tumble through the pages of our books

Tumbleweed Books
HTTP://TUMBLEWEEDBOOKS.CA
An imprint of DAOwen Publications

Teenage Runaway / Ronald J Schulz
ISBN 978-1-998029-29-7
EISBN 978-1-998029-30-3

This is a memoir. Names, characters, places, and incidents are the product of the author's memory and recorded to the best of his ability to be actual persons, living or dead, businesses, companies, events, or locales recreated to the best of his ability. Permission to use legal names were obtained when possible. If permission was not received, the individual(s) name was changed.

Cover art by MMT Productions

10 9 8 7 6 5 4 3 2 1

EDITORS NOTE

This work contains descriptions of events that happened in the late 1960s, and are accurate from the viewpoint of the author. Due to this, some events may not fully coincide with recorded history of those events. This work also contains depictions of racial bias experienced by the author.

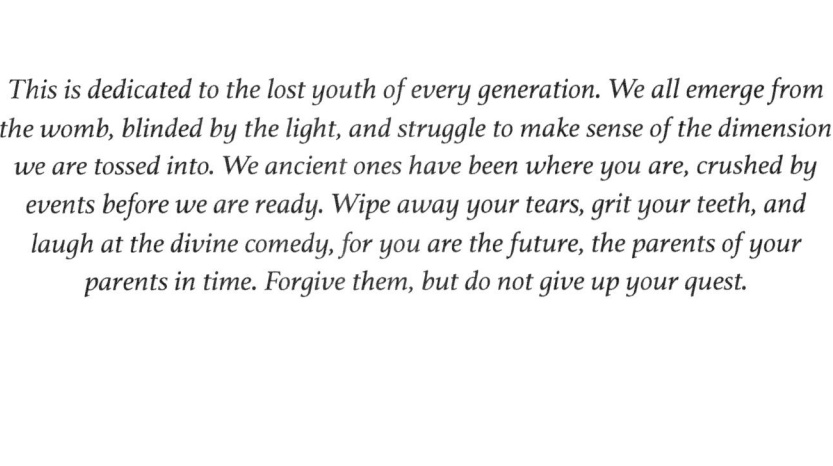

This is dedicated to the lost youth of every generation. We all emerge from the womb, blinded by the light, and struggle to make sense of the dimension we are tossed into. We ancient ones have been where you are, crushed by events before we are ready. Wipe away your tears, grit your teeth, and laugh at the divine comedy, for you are the future, the parents of your parents in time. Forgive them, but do not give up your quest.

HISTORICAL REFERENCE

In the United States, during 1967, police arrested 129,532 runaways - an increase over the 1966 figure of 101,821 and the 1965 figure of 82,198.

Huckleberries for Runaways, by Rev. Larry Beggs
Ballantine, NY. 1969

1

SEPTEMBER 1966: FRESHMAN AT
FENTON HIGH SCHOOL

Ray and Gary walked while I limped beside them. We headed east along the railroad tracks to Fenton from Wood Dale, Illinois. As *almost* adults, we went by ourselves instead of being escorted by our parents to register for class, but the endless riffing of my friends about who had the bigger dick got on my nerves.

Bleach blond Ray beamed his angelic smile as he said, "My cock is so big that I have to tuck the end into my shoe."

"Oh, yeah?" Gary said with a big smirk on his face. "I have to roll mine three times around my waist or I'll trip over it."

"Jeez, guys," I said. "Who the fuck cares about your imaginary cocks? Anyway, we're almost there."

Gary elbowed me. "Remember what I told you, man. Seniors pick on freshmen. They'll call us *fish* and try to trick us."

"They'll even offer to sell you cheap elevator tickets," Ray said with his straight face. I never knew when to believe him.

Gary nodded. "It's true. My brother told me all about it. Don't buy anything from a senior."

"Of course," I said. "There is no elevator at Fenton; everything is on the same floor!"

We all burst out laughing, even though it wasn't funny. Laughing was our release of tension, and Ray's antics always put me in stitches. High school was both exciting and a terrifying challenge for us. All the bullies we knew would be there, bigger, stronger, and with plenty of others we hadn't met. Fenton was infamous for hazing freshmen and for spontaneous fistfights breaking out in the halls.

We lived in Wood Dale, which didn't have a high school, and so after we graduated from the eighth grade, we went to Fenton in the much larger, neighboring town of Bensenville. Over the summer, we'd already scoped it out. It was huge, compared to Highland Junior High, where we three had met in Wood Dale. Fenton had well over a thousand students in our freshman class alone. Most, besides our Wood Dale familiars, would remain anonymous to us.

The railroad tracks were the most direct route from Wood Dale by foot, about two and a half miles from my house. Although I had been warned by my parents about the danger of the railroad tracks, I thought it was safer than the muddy, narrow shoulder along Irving Park, which didn't have sidewalks. Ever since I'd been old enough to leave my yard, I'd wandered along these tracks. The blasting horn of an on-coming train gave us plenty of time to get off to the side. However, we had to step over the occasional pile of shit and toilet paper buzzing with flies that we sometimes found smack in the middle of the tracks.

The toilets on the trains dumped their contents untreated onto the ground. When I rode the train, I looked down when I flushed to see an aluminum plate open as a swirl of water rinsed the contents to the tracks below, and I'd see the railroad ties whizzing by before the plate shut again.

After we crossed under the Route 83 overpass, a well-worn path veered to the right. Following it, we cut across the school's football fields, while the railroad tracks continued running along the north edge of Fenton to the Chicago Loop.

At the beginning of summer, I had answered an ad in the back of a comic book for a Martial Arts training manual. It proclaimed that aikido was far superior to judo or karate at using an opponent's force against him, and you didn't have to be big and strong to beat an oversize attacker. Ray, Gary, and I looked forward to learning enough aikido to trounce the bullies in high school. We practiced in Ray's backyard, without mats, but before we'd had time to run through the initial moves and practice safe landing on the ground, he grabbed and threw me without warning. *Wham!* I landed hard on my right thigh.

As I tried to stand up, pain shot through my right thigh. "Oh, crap! I can't raise my leg." By using my hands, I managed to lift it off the ground and it popped and crackled as I dropped it back down.

Trying to hide his worried look, Ray said, "It's just a sprain, man, it'll go away, eventually."

"But I've got to get in training for Cross-Country track in a few weeks."

Some of my tendons were probably misaligned from that hard fall, but I had to suck it up and stick to my self-imposed training. I'd already decided to run away from home the next spring, and getting in shape for Cross-Country was an important part of my plan, although I didn't tell any of the guys about it.

Ray and Gary were my best friends, but I knew from experience that friends could turn on you, or thoughtlessly spill some secret that could embarrass you or ruin your plans. After being alone so much of my childhood, I had learned to rely more on myself and be wary of others, even when I was an accepted part of a group. The lyrics of Simon and Garfunkel's song, *I Am a Rock,* spoke to me.

I am alone, I am an island... a fortress deep and mighty... I have my books and my poetry to protect me...

Yeah, a rock, that's what I was. Or maybe I was more of a peninsula, not fully connected to anyone's inner circle, although I still enjoyed companionship when I could find it. So I gritted my teeth and pushed myself through the pain, limping through my self-imposed training regimen for the remainder of that summer as Ray and Gary biked alongside, urging me on. My leg's range of motion gradually improved, although by the time school and Cross-Country began in the fall, I still couldn't raise my leg more than halfway off the ground without using my hands. For more than ten years thereafter, I would continue to hear a crackling sound whenever I raised and lowered my right leg.

Fenton had been built in 1956, when I was four. Shiny white tiles with brown trim characterized the modern exterior. Large picture windows let in sunlight along the outside of each classroom, with a small central courtyard with a few manicured shrubs that students could criss-cross on their way to their next class.

We three boys found the halls crowded when we arrived to register. Full of sharks looking for fish. A bigger boy's face exhibited mock sincerity as he blocked our way.

"Hey kid, I got a deal for ya. Wanna buy an elevator ticket? It's only fifty cents." We gave him no answer. "Okay, okay, how about a quarter?"

The rumors were true. We squeezed past him, but farther down the hall, a mob of greasers, in nylon shirts and their hair slicked back, blocked our way. They appraised us with hostile faces, grouped around a much bigger, heavier guy, whose arms were beefier than my legs.

Ray grabbed my shoulder and whispered, "Aw, shit, it's Big John! Let's get outta here!"

This was my first encounter with the legendary Big John Wayne. He looked massive. I was a beanpole, and he could make three of me. The hit song Big John, by Jimmy Dean popped into my head: "Everybody knew you didn't give no lip to big John."

An evil leer crossed his face. "Hey, creeps. Stick around. We wanna have some fun with you."

Here was our chance to show off our aikido moves if only we had made it past the first two lessons. Although we'd talked about standing together against guys like these, Ray and Gary bolted just in time. With my bum leg, I decided running was chicken shit and tried to stand my ground. But when they closed in around me, I saw how futile it was and lost my nerve.

Big John smiled widely at his companions. "Hey, guys, we got us a fresh fish."

They began pushing me from one to the other.

"Cut it out." My voice cracked and sounded weak, embarrassing me.

A lanky guy sneered. "You *wanna* make me, dipshit?" A loose strand of his greasy blond hair hung over his pimple-pocked face.

Big John smirked as he gave them an order. "Tell the wimp to sit down and take off his shoes."

The blond brought his nose up to an inch of mine and his eyes bore into me as he shoved me back against the wall. "You heard the man you jag-off. Sit down and take off your fucking shoes."

A dark-haired greaser held his fist up to my face, and said, "Unless you want a taste of this."

Choosing the lesser evil, I sat down with as much dignity as my situation allowed and untied my gym shoes. John and his minions watched with satisfied smirks.

"That's better, punk," John said. "Now tie them together and hang the laces around your neck." They howled with glee after I'd done so. "Now get the fuck out of our sight, dipshit."

In stocking feet, I hurried off, castigating myself for not fighting back. I'd have gotten creamed, sure, but it was what a guy was supposed to do, regardless of his chance to succeed. Although I had handled myself okay in minor altercations with my classmates, I had never been in a serious fistfight and feared that my inept performance would haunt my reputation. After turning the corner, I jammed my shoes back on. A shred of confidence returned as I saw my friends coming back for me.

"What the hell happened?" Gary said, as if concerned.

Ray only laughed. "Next time, you'll know better. Nobody messes with Big John unless he's crazy or suicidal."

We finally made it to the registration office. A man in a suit with his hair cut into a tight, gray flat-top grabbed my arm, a look of disgust on his face.

"Our school has a dress code, young man. You boys will have to go get your hair cut before you can register for class. I don't want to see any of this Beatle mop top crap. Your hair and sideburns can't be lower than from here to here." He touched the middle of my ear and moved his finger across my cheek to the tip of my nose.

He scrutinized us closer. "And your shirts will have to be tucked in at all times. Hear me? You had better hurry to make it back in time for us to take pictures for your ID cards."

Ray looked perplexed. "ID cards? Jeez, I didn't expect that."

We hurried back down the tracks to Roy's Barber shop, next to Sievers' Drug store in Wood Dale, and made it back in time for our photos. I hated the picture of the gangly youth that appeared on my ID card. It was the face of a wimp who deserved to be pushed around, but my humiliation and misery were only beginning.

Hair was cool. I wanted to identify as a hippie, not the luckless schmuck that I was, but I'd have to escape the conservative world I grew up in to become who I wanted to be.

Ray sighed. "What a bummer. I heard that the dress code down at Addison Trail High isn't nearly as strict as ours."

Garry shook his shorn head. "Girls at Fenton have to wear full skirts, no bare midriffs. If it's cold outside, they can wear pants under their dress going to school but have to take them off in the bathroom before class. If a cheerleader dyes her hair, she gets kicked off the team."

2

FIRST PERIOD STUDY HALL

The school bus dropped me at Fenton's front entrance, where Ray and I clowned around until the first bell rang. That put me in excellent spirits as we parted ways to go to our different classes. My first period was study hall, giving me an hour's break before my school day even began. It was in the library, which was half filled with long tables in front and rows of bookshelves filling the back.

The teacher-monitor demanded silence, but even her stern, pinched face struck me as hilarious. Barely able to contain myself, I took my seat at the long table, with a cute girl on either side of me. The seat across from me was empty until a shadow passed over it as the last bell rang. I looked up to see the hulking figure of Big John pull out the chair and sit there.

He fixed me in an unblinking gaze, with a lazy smirk playing at the corners of his mouth. I had to look away, but even then, under the heat of his baleful gaze, it took me a moment to stifle my giddiness as I tried to focus on my textbooks.

"Hey kid," Big John said, and waited for me to glance up at him. "You are ugly. Hear me? *Ug-ly*, and a real jag-off, too." He spoke in a low tone, but I heard him alright, and so did the girls. They giggled and shot me contemptuous glances, whether or not they knew that jag-off meant masturbator.

Big John was just warming up. "Look at me when I'm talking to you, punk. You hear me, don't you? You're nothing but a piece of shit. I'm talking to *you*, dipshit."

I felt his eyes boring into me. Summoning my flagging courage, I looked up for another second at his scowling face of pure evil, proof of how much he relished his power to degrade and humiliate me. I could feel my face blanching under his hot gaze.

"You are a jag off," he repeated over and over like a sing-song lullaby. His whispered words of hate were certainly not a remedy for my jagged nerves. The teacher, sitting primly at her desk, didn't pay him any attention, and I wondered if she had deliberately sent him to harass me on my first day of high school.

I found no answer to why he hated me so much, whether it was my giddy sense of humor, or my face that he insisted was so ugly, although his hateful mug wouldn't win any beauty prize. The expected hour of peaceful contemplation had turned into a grueling ordeal. He could ruin my whole semester if I had to face him every day. The bell finally rang, and I scooted out ahead of him, limping on my bum leg, and made my way to my next class. My mind was absorbed by my predicament as I passed an ordinary-looking boy.

Wham! I turned around to see that the boy had been slammed against the lockers, where he was pinned, wide-eyed, in shock. What surprised me was who did it. Not a greaser, but a balding male teacher in a suit and tie, who screamed at him.

"Tuck that damn shirt in. Do it now! Next time I won't be so gentle."

Wow, they sure didn't cut a guy any slack around here. Fortunately, I'd tucked my shirttail back in only moments before. My fellow students and I were caught between the bullies, most of them greasers, and the pitiless demands of our teachers. I felt like I was a prisoner in one of the Nazi concentration camps I read about. They were harassed by SS guards and also by the capos, or overseers, who were as cruel, despite being prisoners themselves. It was impossible for me to focus on my studies that had nothing to do with my real-life problems.

The first fistfight I saw erupted like spontaneous combustion out of nowhere in the crowded hallway. Books and assignments flew like confetti as two greasers tore into each other. Their fists blurred as they pummeled each other with lightning speed. Someone yelled *a teacher is coming*, and their friends tore them away from each other, abandoning their books and papers for someone else, perhaps a flunky, to gather up. One of them shouted over his shoulder, "We'll finish this under the bridge!"

That, I soon learned, was the usual challenge to a duel and the Route 83 Bridge over the railroad tracks was Fenton's field of honor for formal slug fests. I walked home that way and found the contest was well attended by student spectators, like a boxing match, only with less constraint.

They went at it again, but with less vigor than before. Whatever rage fueled them had dissipated over the long day. After trading a few punches, they grappled in the grass before separating to cuss at each other and then went their separate ways.

Chick Fights, battles between girls, could be as vicious as those between guys. The chicks were usually tough greaser girls with their hair ratted up into a high bouffant that was often a prime target for her opponent to grab and pull. Slapping, kicking, clawing and scratching took the place of masculine punches, but I never saw a Chick Fight conducted under the bridge.

3

SIXTH PERIOD STUDY HALL

That first afternoon, I took a corner seat at the long table assigned to me in the other, purpose-built study hall, with my back to the teacher's desk in front. On my right sat a dusky, dark-eyed girl with exceptionally long black hair. She flashed me a shy smile before her eyes darted back to her book. Brimming with desperate confidence, I introduced myself.

"Hi, I'm Ron. What's your name?"

She giggled, glanced up at me, and then looked away before saying something with an intriguing singsong accent that sounded like *Thiralop* something or other. Students around the table snickered, and I told them to knock it off.

"Where are you from, Thira?"

Her accent threw me. I wasn't sure if she said Thailand or Taiwan, but she was a most unexpected treat, as I'd never met an Asian girl. Aside from a few Mexicans, our suburban neighborhood was composed of Lilly White European descendants, and I welcomed the sight of this exotic beauty. My luck sure had changed for the better since morning study hall.

Before I could ask for more, the bell rang, signaling us to silence. Thira and I shot each other sly glances, and waited for the ending bell to free our soft whispers to comprehensible speech. I wondered how much English she understood and agonized over the best words to use on her. The clock clicked a countdown to the last fifteen minutes. Then a couple of teachers entered the room and approached the study hall monitor, who pointed our way. "She's right over there."

They came to our table and surrounded Thira. "Come with us," one of them said.

She answered my quizzical look with a broad smile and followed them out. Maybe she needed paperwork processed, and I assured myself that she'd be back at our next scheduled study hall and when she wasn't, I assumed she was sick.

Thiraporn Lopwri from Thailand was Fenton's first foreign exchange student. Later on, an announcement over the PA system introduced her and said she'd be putting on a full costume Thai temple dance. I attended both performances in the Little Theatre. It was packed. Her graceful beauty and fluid movements won my adoration. She put an alluring human face on the vast Asian continent that for most of her audience had been limited to news photos of the grimacing soldiers of the yellow peril that some of our politicians said threatened to overwhelm our great country, the land of the free.

It was over a month later that I spotted her in the hall between classes, laughing with a group of Thespians and honor students who surrounded her, as if she was in protective custody. I tried to wave and catch her attention, but she was too hemmed in, or maybe embarrassed, to notice me. Never again did I see her on her own without an insulating covey of better-bred students, who kept her away from riffraff like me. Tough luck hounded me, derailing my chances to make it with girls. This was another reason to escape my hometown for the wider world.

4

SMOKING IN THE JOHN

John Wayne and Big Tom stood smoking by the window in the boy's bathroom when I ran in to take a piss before my next class. They snickered and closed in on me, and each of them was double my weight.

Tom had been my classmate in Wood Dale's elementary school and had always seemed friendly to me back in junior high, which we had graduated from only months before, but he wore an evil sneer on his face as he backed me up against the wall.

"Hey, John, look, it's a dork! Let's have some fun with him."

John chuckled as he leaned against the door, blocking my exit. "Go ahead, Tom." As the leader of the pack, John seemed to enjoy letting his underlings show off their nastiness by terrorizing luckless schmucks like me.

"What do you guys want?" I said, but was disappointed at how weak my voice sounded. At that age; it was prone to cracking under the best of conditions.

"Ha-ha," Tom said as he brought his nose up to mine. "This shit head is shaking. What are you scared of, huh, you panty-waist wimp? I bet you could use a knuckle sandwich. Didja ever have one?"

He almost sounded jocular when he said that, but he put his fist up to my mouth as he turned to John. "I bet this jag-off doesn't even know what a knuckle sandwich is." He shoved his fist in my face. "Do you, jag-off?"

No way could I take on both or either of these brutes. After slamming me up against the wall a couple times, they had a big laugh and left me to take my piss and run to my next class, where I arrived too late to beat the bell.

The teacher sent me to the office for a reprimand and gave me extra homework for coming in late. It could have been worse, and yet I was overwhelmed by feelings of inadequacy because I hadn't handled myself as well as I wished. My nerves, my voice, my body betrayed me, and I was still bound by a reasonable yet unmanly caution. The only way I would ever be respected was to fling myself at the enemy, like a berserk Viking warrior, regardless of the outcome. As a mere victim, I was nothing but a laughingstock, and I couldn't help feeling that it was true. I was just a stupid, all around loser.

This wasn't the last time bullies harassed me. Their contemptuous words killed my spirit. When I looked in the mirror, the face of a total loser stared back at me. The more students and teachers mocked me, the more a loser I became. My dreams were haunted by scenes of the humiliation that awaited me at school. It sapped my energy, my confidence and well-being.

Suicide began to sound like a good option, but my brain screamed *No!* As long as I lived there was hope, but not there in Fenton. I had to get the hell out to reinvent myself as someone I could face in the mirror and be proud of. That was a better solution than suicide, which remained my fallback plan, a way to redeem myself with some samurai honor if I failed to escape this hellhole.

Fifth period algebra was impossible. Miss Nafziger's dreary monotone voice droned on as she drew meaningless symbols on the blackboard. After a few weeks of that, I became incapable of staying awake in class. I sat by the door, leaned my back against the wall and let her monologue lull me to sleep. She must have recognized by then that I was beyond saving and let me be. A long string of Fs was my well-deserved grade, but my naps refreshed my mind, which I needed more than algebra to plan my escape.

Hating school didn't mean I disliked learning. Quite the contrary, I had a profound interest in the larger world, but school wasn't there to satisfy my curiosity or expand my horizons. School was society's boot camp. It hammered us all into the spineless, mindless tools of their society. The system had to stamp out our individuality for us to take our place in the colorless ranks of conservative yes-men. Upon graduating, we would cloth ourselves in military uniforms or business suits, and perhaps marry an insipid wife, a woman like my mother. For that's what Mom, with her drinking, whining, and bitching at Dad, had become. Women too needed their spirits crushed to fit into the role that society expected of them.

As the eldest of her five children, I remembered a happier woman who lit up the room with joy, but that seemed so long ago. It was a sad downward death spiral that I watched as Mom and Dad sank into endless arguments, blaming each other for their meaningless existence, and I wanted no part of what they called success.

Each day of my freshman year made running away more necessary. I'd lost faith in justice, whether legal or cosmic, and I knew better than to trust in a silent God, a blind Fate, or any external power to rescue me. It was up to me alone to act and fulfill my preferred destiny or die trying. My only chance to survive and flourish was to run away from home and school. It was essential for my psychological self-defense. Therefore, I'd make my break for freedom soon after my fifteenth birthday in March, when the weather was warmer and I had a chance to go far away.

5

CROSS-COUNTRY TRACK AND A JOB

By the time school began in the fall of 1966, my summer long running program had improved my right leg's range of motion and I didn't limp as much. Coach Townsend shook his head doubtfully when I showed up for try-outs.

"Okay, son, I'll let you run with the team for a week, but if your leg doesn't improve by then, you will have to drop out. Think you can hack it?"

"Sure, Coach, it's already much better than it was last week."

He ran us up and down the steep hill of excavated earth that remained, as a kind of monument from the school's construction. It was tough going just to keep up with the middle of the herd of running boys, but over the week my limp improved, and most of the pain subsided. But as hard as I pushed myself, I never came in under thirteen minutes, which remained my best run time for the two-mile course. What mattered to me was to be in good enough shape for my runaway journey, not winning awards.

Coach Townsend gathered us together one day and gave us an inspirational speech to highlight what our training could do for us.

"Most of you boys will enlist or be drafted into the Army or Marines in a couple of years. If this war in Vietnam is still going on, you will be sent there, but don't worry if you miss it. By that time, there will always be another conflict to go to. On day you may find yourself cut off in a jungle or a rice paddy, maybe even wounded, with your buddies all dead or run off. There will be no one around to help you. That's when you will have a simple choice, to live or to die, and if you choose to live, you will reach down inside of yourself and pull up the memory of how you pushed yourself here. When you were gasping for air, your legs about to give out, you ran on, giving it your absolute damndest to reach the goal. And that's what will save your lives."

I took his speech to heart and later on, lost in the swamps; it kept me going when I needed to push my limits. I planned to trek through a couple of Illinois counties to make it to a distant town where no one would recognize me and I could buy a ticket to somewhere far away without raising alarm.

After cross-country, I went out for wrestling under Coach Clamp, and did well in practice, but with a screaming, heckling audience, I became dazed, and my moves got slower. Stage fright kept me from winning any matches. My self confidence was at an all-time low, but it could only improve after I escaped the jeering fishbowl of high school.

Then I took a job at Ehlan's Green Tree Inn, right across the railroad tracks from Fenton. It was a popular restaurant that hired students as dishwashers and busboys, including Gary's older brother Bob, who ran through a brief introduction to the job by way of training me.

"This is the ice tea dispenser," he said. "You can help yourself anytime and tell the cook what you want him to make for your one free meal at break time. Oh, and here," he handed me one of two tall glasses of ice tea. "I already prepared these to give you a toast to starting your new job." We clinked our glasses together and shouted, "Cheers!"

Thirsty, I took a big gulp, and it burned my mouth and throat. Bob burst out laughing. "Gotcha, man!" he said. "Did you ever have Tabasco sauce before?"

I had to fill another glass to guzzle some fresh water before I could stop coughing and say anything with a raspy voice. "Hell, no, this is my first time to try it."

Bob beamed at me. "Welcome to the club. Every new guy gets a dose of Tabasco. It's our way of bringing a guy into our team."

Despite the harsh introduction, Tabasco became a lifelong favorite of mine. One of my fellow dishwashers was a super macho, heavy smoker in his mid twenties who bragged that he just got out of the Marines.

"That's where the real men go," he said. "The regular Army is for wimps." He rolled up his sleeve to his shoulder. "See this, kid?" He had a globe of the world with an anchor super imposed over it and "Semper Fi," inked in below. Translated from Latin, it means "always faithful."

He slammed his fist against his chest. "The Marines make you goddamned tough if you can survive it. A couple of our men didn't even survive basic training."

He chuckled and his eyes bugged out like a maniac, as if he was trying to psyche me out. "We had to crawl about a hundred feet under barbed wire while they fired live rounds from an M60 machine gun above our heads. Two guys snapped. They started screaming and stood up. Fuck, they got torn to shreds, man. You just don't do something stupid like that and deserve to live."

Ehlan's Green Tree Inn was my first paying job. I liked the work and the rough camaraderie with the guys, who played practical jokes on each other as well as me. My fellow dishwashers and I not only got a free meal, we scrounged plenty of leftover food, too. Some of the pampered elites we served didn't even touch a whole plate of steak or shrimp with all the trimmings, so it came back to the kitchen to be gobbled by us as we stacked dirty dishes on the dishwasher conveyer belt. I worked after school a few nights a week and on the weekends until past midnight at kid's wages.

The job helped me earn enough money to be a runaway success. I would need to buy bus tickets, meals and pay rent as I set up my new life somewhere far away from the dreary place I called home.

6

WINTER 1966: COACH CLAMP'S HEALTH CLASS

Ever since we were in junior high, seventh and eighth grades, boys and girls had separate gym classes, but in high school, we also had gym uniforms, shorts and an orange tee shirt emblazoned with a bison, our school mascot. We even had gym lockers and took showers before changing back into our street clothes for the next class. In the last quarter of the year, gym became Coach Clamp's health class for boys, a euphemism for Sex Ed. It was held in a regular classroom, and we didn't need to change or shower afterwards.

Coach was trim and muscular, a man's man. He was beloved by his male students, even the dorkiest of losers like me. He peppered his lectures with sardonic humor and relished telling us tales of his glory days as a Marine serving in Korea and Japan.

"We had a terrific time in Korea. We hung chains under our chopper and flew low over the tall grass and rice fields, flushing out whole flocks of pheasants. As they flew up, we blew them away with our machine-gun. What a blast we had, and it was excellent gunnery practice for the guys."

I raised my hand. "Did you gather them up to eat afterwards?" Some of the jocks and greasers chortled at such a dumb question.

"What?" he said, looking startled by the outlandish idea. "No, our fifty-caliber machine guns tore them to shit, not worth our trouble."

It bothered me that he bragged about such wonton carnage and waste, but I needed to hear more of his stories.

"Old Korean men wear these miniature stovepipe hats, too small for their heads. They look ridiculous. As we flew up on an unsuspecting old man, doddering along, the guys took bets on whether the gunner could make the shot."

Mr. Clamp's audience of fourteen-year-old boys was rapt, eager to hear what came next. He slammed his right fist into his left palm and said, "Pow! A single shot took off the geezer's hat. He looked around, wondering where the hell it went, before scampering away like the devil was after him. It was hilarious! Man, do I ever miss the fun we had in Korea. You boys should enlist in the Marines after you graduate; I guarantee that it will make real men out of you."

A boy raised his hand. "What if he missed the hat and killed the old man?"

That brought a sly smile to Clamp's face. "Well, I guess that would be the old man's piss poor luck, now, wouldn't it?"

I couldn't imagine any of my other teachers describing escapades like these, but Mr. Clamp was just warming up. He got to the all-important theme of his class: sex. First, he went over the fundamentals. Using charts and slides, he mapped out the body parts and biological changes in the male and female bodies that we were all experiencing. It was dry and academic, and I'd heard it all before. When he got to the juicy part, my ears picked up.

"Now I'm sure you boys already know how it works by now, and you better be careful not to get a girl pregnant. There are plenty of things you can do to get your fun, without shooting off in her pussy."

Embarrassed laughter rippled through the room.

"We'll call it a vagina here. Got me? For God's sakes, always wear a rubber! You may think you're in love, but you boys and whatever girl you're with doesn't need to be saddled with a squalling kid just yet."

"No, sir!" the class answered resoundingly, as was expected of us.

"If your girlfriend keeps putting you off, won't let you make it to third base, and then, suddenly one night when her parents are gone, she's hot to trot and begging you for it. You damn well better stop right there and run out of the door!"

He paused for dramatic effect, looking around the room, especially at his star athletes on the football team. Like the rest of us, their mouths were hanging open in anticipation.

"Why, you may ask?" He paced before the blackboard, building anticipation in his audience. And then his voice roared. "Because that is the worst time of the month to fuck her! Your girl is ovulating. That means that she's in heat. Her body is telling her that she needs to get pregnant right now. So, you better stick it anywhere but in her vagina. Go away and come back in a couple of days when she's not ovulating. Got me?"

Coach Clamp was outspoken and sympathetic to us horny males. He knew his guys needed to get laid; they only had to be careful about it.

"It's a damn shame that prostitution is illegal in this country, because that could save you boys a ton of grief. It's legal in some countries, like Japan, where I had the best sex of my life. We spent our leaves in the Yokosuka Red-Light district when I was stationed there. The Mama-San was my best friend. We'd bring her presents of booze, cigarettes and chocolates and party away our whole liberty."

The class sat in rapt attention, as silent as if we were at church, as Mr. Clamp continued.

"We had a guy in our unit with the biggest dick I ever saw on a white man. He was a simple-minded hillbilly, not very bright, and he didn't go in for foreplay. He just charged over and rammed that thing into a poor working girl, like *ready or not, here I come,* and he'd bang away like there was no tomorrow without thinking about how she felt about it."

He let his excited class settle down. "Let me tell you, the girls were not happy with him, so Mama-San and I decided we'd teach him a valuable lesson. I asked her to find the girl with the tightest pussy in the district. She found one tighter than a virgin and we all chipped in, paid her plenty extra, so we could pull a surprise birthday party on 'ol Big Dick.

"The walls in Japan, you see, are made of paper. We had his lovely present waiting for him, spread-eagled on the futon with a bow tied around her middle, while the Mama-San waited with us with the rest of her girls on the other side of the paper wall, watching the shadow play through the paper. We had all we could do to keep from laughing out loud as Big Dick came in with the biggest hard-on you ever saw. From the far end of the room, he charged like a raging bull at the poor girl, but when he plowed into her, we heard a big scream, and it wasn't from the girl. That's what we were waiting for.

"We punched through the paper wall, shouting *Surprise!* He was doubled over; screaming in pain, blood everywhere, and it was all his blood. She wasn't exactly laughing, no, but she was in on our game and glad to see him get what he deserved. He had split his cock wide open trying to ram it into her. We all had a good laugh at that dumb hillbilly. He had a stupid grin on his face too, but it took him over a week to laugh with us.

"We'd brought along our medic and, drunk as he was, he got into the spirit of things. He took all the bandages he had with him, wrapped Big Dick's cock until it was as big as a basketball. We couldn't zipper up his pants, and had to leave that white mummy of a monster sticking out for the entire world to see. You can imagine what he looked like the next morning, standing in formation with this huge white basketball sticking out of his pants, and a big dumb grin on his face."

Coach Clamp slapped his thigh and the whole room cracked up. He easily won over all the boys with his lessons illustrated by stories from his wide experience. Then he wound back to the therapeutic part of his lesson.

"Now, boys, this brings us to what is called honeymoon rape. Some guys, not me, of course, want some pure, unblemished virgin as their bride. Maybe he also has no hands-on experience with sex. There they are, two ignorant kids, stupidly, deeply in love. But after the wedding, he's so horny, maybe drunk as well, anxious for the big moment. The knot is tied. It's all legal now, she's finally all his. What do you suppose happens?"

The class murmured comments like, "He fucks her, doesn't he?"

Coach Clamp shook his head with a bemused smile on his face. "No, the poor bastard has no idea that she needs to get warmed up, doesn't even understand that a girl has to get turned on to have a wet pussy. It is her lubrication to let his dick slide in, and she probably has no idea about it, either. But he has to break her maidenhead before he can get it in. So, like that dumb hillbilly, he rams it in, causing her pain as he busts her cherry wide open just to get his rocks off."

He looked around the room with a sardonic smile. "Think she had any fun? He probably just rolls over and goes to sleep while she's lying there in pain, bleeding. From that point on, she hates sex. Can you blame her? All too often, it becomes a marriage on the rocks. Let me tell you, a real man has got to understand a woman's sex drive." He crossed his arms over his chest, like he was in a Mr. Clean commercial, and nodded. "Oh, yes, they want it too, just like you."

Coach Clamp was like a character from one of the men's magazines my friends and I found buried deep in our fathers' closets, and he was never boring. His bragging about massacring birds, or shooting the hats off old Korean men, upset my sense of fair play, but I was thrilled by his whorehouse tales.

That's where I belonged, a man among men and surrounded by vivacious, sex mad women, living a life of wild adventure in exotic locations all around the world. Only the military seemed to hold out that kind of opportunity for me, and I didn't care which Army it was. As I was too young for my country's service, maybe I could enlist overseas in the French Foreign Legion or in the Israeli Army. I'd read the book, Exodus, and figured that Israel, surrounded by enemies, needed manpower, and therefore should be less picky about accepting anonymous recruits, whether underage or not.

7

FAMILY LIFE

When I heard the car come up the driveway, I snapped to attention, stuck the book I was reading under the mattress, and slipped out of my room. Dad hated to find me in my room. He insisted I spent too much time reading. I had to be outside, raking leaves, picking up fallen apples, or doing one of the never-ending chores he demanded of me. My free time after school, and on the weekends, had to be gainfully employed, which limited my opportunity to socialize with friends. Other boys had time to hang out with their friends, but most of them lived a mile away on the other side of town.

As a do-it-yourself workaholic, Dad didn't have time to toss a ball around after work, because he was forever remodeling the house or landscaping the yard. I never had a chance to develop the baseball skills my classmates did over the summer, making me an unwelcome loser they didn't want on their team when school resumed.

Dad's straight faced greeting to me was always the same. "What have you accomplished today, Ronnie?"

Accomplished, how I hated that word. No matter how often we'd gone through that ritual greeting, I never felt comfortable answering.

On the surface, it seemed innocuous, but his tone presumed that I was just a lazy, irresponsible kid, humiliating me.

"Oh, nothing special, Dad. I'm just picking up the apples." I bent my back to it, pretending I'd been at it since I'd gotten home from school. What, I wondered, could be wrong with my response this time? No matter how fast or long I worked, apples kept falling until there were no more.

"Hmm." He kicked around deep in the crabgrass to unearth a half rotten apple and then another. "I see that you missed a few over here. You always do such a slipshod job, Ronnie," he said with a sigh of resignation. "Some son I've got. When will you be a boy that I can be proud of?"

If that was the extent of today's lecture, he'd step inside. Mom began loudly banging pots and slamming doors as soon as he appeared. Before Dad came home, she was cheerful, even cracking jokes, or asking me how my day went at school. With my sisters and me, she had normal human conversation. When Dad came home, she transformed into a bitch.

Her phony voice dripped with bitter sarcasm. "Hello *dear*, how did your day go at work?"

"*Ma-ther*," Dad said wearily, drawing out her title. "What the Sam Hill is the problem now?"

"*Prob-lem*?" Her voice started out ridiculously low and then rose into the caricature of a squeaky, high-pitched girl. "I don't have a problem. Do you see a problem around here?"

"Come on *dear*, can't we just have a civil conversation for once? For God's sakes, I support you. You have a damn roof over your head. Why can't you be a regular wife and appreciate me as a man?"

Her eyes got big, feigning surprise. "A man? I don't see a *real* man around here. Let me know if you find one."

Dinnertime put a hold on their skirmish. "Come on, kids, let's eat!" Dad called out.

My five younger sisters and I sat down and ate the meatloaf or casserole and a single dish of overcooked vegetables. The six o'clock news stayed on throughout the meal, a welcome distraction from Mom's continued whiny remarks.

"Can I have some milk?" My sister Suzy said as the full plastic gallon jug was near me, I took the initiative and began pouring it into her cup. Dad watched me like a hawk.

"You're going to spill it," he said with authority. "Watch it! You're going to spill it, I said."

"Watch what?" I yelled back in exasperation. "I've poured milk many times when you weren't around, Dad. I'm fourteen, not a kid anymore."

That was true, but like a sorcerer's incantation, Dad's words and expectations cast a spell on me, and I lost control over my muscles. I watched the level rising in the cup but was unable to stop pouring. It overflowed before I could somehow regain control of my arm and set it down.

"See, I told you!" Dad said triumphantly. "Why don't you ever listen to me, Ronnie? Now get a dishrag and clean it up."

Dad's negative expectations shook me up, shattering my self-confidence. If I didn't get away from him, I'd never be anything but a loser. My family was simmering in a stew pot of passive hostility.

Dinner over, Dad retreated to the basement or garage, where he had innumerable projects to keep his hands busy late into the night. *Idle hands are the devil's workshop* was his motto, and he'd drag me down with him.

"Help me with this now and you can finish your homework later," he said insistently.

He yelled, swore at un-cooperative bolts, and lost track of time. I could be there, like a loyal minion, until past midnight. It was worse on the weekends, when I had no excuse, like schoolwork or bedtime, to get away from him. And so it went. Mom's words dripping poisonous sarcasm and Dad relentlessly riding my ass. I'd started out being the "good kid." Obeying my parents, teachers, and ministers, however, I came to learn that being good made me irrelevant, someone to take for granted and push around. Their plans for my future lacked one vital ingredient – *me*.

8

FATHER AND SON TALKS

Dad lay under the jacked-up car with me kneeling beside him on the cold concrete in the garage. He'd been banging on a jammed bolt when he suddenly stopped, took a deep breath, and exhaled his words with excruciatingly slow deliberation.

"You, ah, know, Ronnie, that your, ah, mom has, ahhhh, problems."

It took so long for him to get out a simple sentence that I was always tempted to jump in and finish it for him. I was usually correct in knowing what he wanted to say; however, I'd learned to bite my tongue. My personality rankled him as much as his did me.

"She... can be so... *un-rea-son-able*... at times." He'd finally got that out and sped up a bit. "Sometimes, you know, I just don't know how to handle her."

At least he was confiding in me, talking to me as a person instead of an incompetent servant. It didn't take much to understand that Mom was not a happy woman. When he was home, she'd drink, throw tantrums, bitch and moan and wordlessly slam doors as she passed through the house.

Mom was nothing like the suburban moms on television, the June Cleavers on Leave it to Beaver. None of the television couples like

Ozzie and Harriet ever had serious conflicts or jobs they hated. I was convinced that all these 'make work' projects that Dad busied himself with, and pulled me into, were just his escape from Mom, and not a wise solution to his problems. They rarely went out and didn't socialize with anyone but my grandparents. The solution seemed simple.

"Take her out to dinner, Dad, spend more time with her."

"I've tried to." His voice sounded weary. "You know, I made dinner reservations last week. I even bought her roses, and you saw what she did. 'Who brought these ugly things?' she said and threw them straight into the garbage can. Then she refused to change out of her robe or fix her hair. Finally, I canceled the reservations."

I remembered watching that sad affair play out. As a teenager, there was only so much marital advice I could give, but I was a realist. If the darn thing didn't work, end it. I took a deep breath and laid it on the line.

"Maybe you and Mom ought to get divorced?"

Dad didn't answer straightaway. He picked up his hammer and got back to work on that stubborn bolt. I'd overheard them talking late one night and the 'D' word had been uttered.

Dad finally sighed and put down his tools. "You know, Ronnie. People in our family just don't get divorced. That's the easy way out." He shifted his position under the car and let out another deep sigh. "Get me that other wrench over there, will you? No! Not that one. Pay attention to what's going on. Will you? Give me that other one."

Our meaningful talk was over. It was back to nuts and bolts. Dad kept himself swamped with mindless, busy work. He was miserable in his office job, married to a shrew, while Mom kept herself zoned out with booze. Sure, I loved Mom, but her strategy was flawed with soul crushing negativity. My parents avoided facing and fixing their reality and nothing I said or did could improve their situation. If I didn't get away from them, I might turn into my father, which would be a fate worse than death.

The only future I envisioned with any kind of joy was to join the Army or Marines and see the world.

9

THE SUMMER OF LOVE

April 5, 1967: San Francisco City officials are worried that they will be inundated with young people when schools across the country let out for the summer. The Council for the Summer of Love has put out a news release, warning about overcrowding and potential health and safety hazards.

T hanks to television news coverage, the word was out, even in the suburban village of Wood Dale. San Francisco was becoming the great Mecca for alienated youth and 1967 would be forever known as the "Summer of Love." There seemed to be a welcoming community out in California, and it encouraged me that I wasn't the only one trying to break free.

The hippie subculture was sprouting free-flowing Flower Power out of the staid, dry concrete of the American cultural landscape, and I was desperate to join it. Runaways flocked to Haight-Ashbury and Golden Gate Park, but so did the police, hunting them down. News reports and magazine articles told me that cops combed the bus and train stations for newly arriving underage kids. With reluctance, I crossed San Francisco off my list of destinations.

New Orleans captivated me after I read *The French Quarter: an informal history of the New Orleans underworld*, by Herbert Asbury. It was an old book and had a lot of unfamiliar words, difficult reading for me at that time, but the depictions of the red-light districts, like Storyville, enticed me with the promise of available sex. That, along with basic survival, and blending in as an adult, was uppermost in my mind.

New Orleans wasn't in the news as a runaway destination, and it was a Gulf port city where I might get a job on the docks or even hop a freighter to lands beyond. In my dreams I led a life like those in the paperback books and men's magazines I devoured, but enough of fantasy. I needed to experience that life of adventure and so I buckled down, working to make it happen.

By the end of 1966, I made one hundred and seven bucks at Ehlan's. It wasn't much when minimum wage for a kid was under a dollar an hour. That gave me a reason to quit the wrestling team, so I dropped out to work longer and earn more money. Our wrestling coaches tried to pressure us into starving ourselves down to lower weight classes, which was a losing strategy for me. I was thin and needed to bulk up, rather than wear myself down. Also, it was Christmas, and I wanted to relax and enjoy one last holiday before I ran off into an uncertain future. However, my nostalgic longing for a last merry Christmas with my family was soon dashed. Helping him in the basement, Dad harangued me.

"What the heck did you quit wrestling for? You didn't go out for baseball or football, like I suggested. You did pretty well in track, although I would have preferred it if you chose basketball. I got a letter sweater, you know, when I was your age. Now you're just a quitter. All you do is in half measures, Ronnie. You will never succeed at anything if you don't put your mind to it."

He tossed the wrench back on the disorganized heap of tools that covered his workbench and threw his hands up with a loud sigh of exasperation. "Why can't you be more like your cousin Davy? He's a *real* boy, excels in sports, and doesn't waste his time reading all that *garbage* you do."

Cousin Davy was two years older than me, and no saint. He lived in a neighborhood packed with boys his age. His dad, my dad's twin, was quiet and didn't storm around the house yelling like mine did. I wished my dad was more like Davy's, but there was another side to this.

Dad's voice softened. "When I was a kid, Ronnie, my dad always said Ed was the smarter one, not me. Sure, Ed got better grades. They sent him to officer's school in the Army, made him a lieutenant in a machinegun company before sending him to fight Hitler, but our dad, your grandpa, God rest his soul, said I couldn't do anything right. Whenever I couldn't figure out a math problem or spell a word, Dad yelled *Dummkopf* at me."

He looked at me with big, wounded eyes, which told me that the harsh word spoken decades ago in his youth still rankled. It must have reverberated in his brain, sapping his self-esteem, just like his words did to me.

Dad shook his head. "You know, Ronnie, your grandma was born in Germany and my dad, your grandpa, was a second-generation Kraut." A little chuckle escaped him before he shook his head and sucked in a lungful of air. "I only learned the bad words in German. Our folks spoke English to us kids around the house, but they spoke German to each other when they didn't want us to know."

That helped me understand Dad better. He was still trying to prove himself to his long-dead father. While he also called me *Dummkopf*, he usually called me *oddball*, or *weirdo*. He called me lazy, too, especially when I had a tough time staying attentive to some grueling, late-night project that he corralled me into. It struck me that this negative energy could pass down, father to son, into future generations, unless I cut the link and created a new, more positive legacy.

A slur may not affect everyone the same way. Dad's yelling got to me more than my sisters. It felt as if my manhood was at stake, but my sisters found his angry words titillating, especially when they were directed at Mom. They tended to take his side against her regardless, as if unable to see themselves in her place.

Words may not break bones, but they sure can break spirits. Dad didn't realize that he was doing the same to me as his father had done to him. Pleasing Dad was a hopeless task, and I gave up trying. Dad's lecturing voice droned on, even in my nightmares.

"Think of your future," he'd say. "Today's industry is looking to the future. Nowadays, you need a good education to get a good job. Look at all the advantages I've given you. You have a chance to go to college and buy a home of your own. You could be even more successful than I've been."

I didn't want to be successful, not for what it cost him. He hated his job, and I'd seen where he worked. It was a large smoky room lit by florescent lights, filled with slanted tables covered in schematic diagrams. He was a rank below a full-fledged draftsman, wearing a suit and tie that he tore off as soon as he got home. What he did looked lifeless and boring to me. It must have constrained him as much as it would have me, although he'd never admit it.

As for college, I got mixed messages. Dad hated the *college boys* who got promoted over him with no work experience. Dad could have used the GI Bill after he got out of the Navy, but he only managed an associate degree that he paid for himself. It was something about proving himself by paying his own way. His lack of education, or talking skills, seemed to bar him from promotion at his job. From interpreting the garbled explanations that I got from him, I began to realize that Dad was covering up his own feelings of inadequacy. I could sympathize because I felt the same way. We could have been buddies if he'd only leveled with me. Good old Dad. What could I do without him? I would succeed by living my life my way.

10

FINAL PREPARATIONS

By March 1967, I'd made four hundred more dollars. Mom pressured me to bank the lot of it, but I gave her only a token amount and hid the rest in a cubbyhole in my dresser. Ever rummaging through my stuff, Mom found and banked most of it in an account that I couldn't access until I was eighteen. Devastated, I pushed back my departure to when I'd have at least two hundred and fifty dollars in hand. That would have to do until I found a place to live and a way to make more.

Inspired by the heroes in my books, I created a fictitious identity. For a first name, I stuck with Jim, my true middle name. Hassel, the author and principal character of my beloved book Comrades of War, would do for a last name. Jim Hassel – it had a nice ring to it. I practiced saying it over and over to be ready to respond when called upon. It wouldn't do for me to give myself away by answering late.

My fictional hometown had to be somewhere in the Midwest, so my accent, or lack thereof, wouldn't give me away. Secret agents had to memorize trivial details of their fictional identities, like street names, work history, places they supposedly went to school or worked. That took a lot of research, and I didn't have all the info for any town but my own. There wasn't a war on, people weren't looking for spies, and I doubted that an interrogator would grill me as close as the Gestapo would. That was an oversight that would become my undoing.

Failure to succeed on my first attempt could mean reform school, the boy's jail over in St. Charles, across the Fox River. So, like the military operations I read about, I planned my escape in total secrecy. Even my closest friends had to be kept in the dark. I'd read enough about spy-craft and knew how easy it was for someone to let something slip and endanger the lives of an entire espionage network, therefore I remained a network of one. My plan included misinformation, little clues I left behind to misdirect the police.

Expo '67 would open in Montréal, Canada on April 27, 1967. Millions of people were expected to attend and I might be able to lose myself in the crowd, so I carefully traced out a route via Chicago to Montréal on one of my maps from the gas station. They used to offer these fold-out maps free of charge and I had almost a complete collection covering the United States and Canada.

But I had no intention of going to Montréal and I hid my map under the large writing pad on my desk, as if I didn't want it found. It was part of my deception plan. Because if they spent all their time looking for me where I wasn't, I stood a better chance of getting away in the opposite direction. By the middle of May, I was as ready and desperate as I could be to escape from my personal hell and create my new identity as a confident, grown up man of the world.

11

MONDAY, MAY 15, 1967

For hours I lay awake in the darkness, my heart pounding, eager for the sunrise. This was to be the day. I would run away or die trying. I couldn't endure another day of waiting and my stomach was knotted with anxiety, but if I got up too early, it would look suspicious. Finally, my alarm clock went off. After planning my escape for over a year, it was time to jump into action.

The day would be bright and clear, an ordinary spring day and as good as any to run for my life. Mom, as usual, wasn't up yet, and I got ready on my own. I dressed for school and stuffed myself with an egg and toast breakfast, and a tall glass of strawberry flavored Carnation Instant Breakfast, probably my last hot meal for a long while. Although in expectation of a warm day, I was wearing two long-sleeved shirts, layered over each other, and an equal number of pants.

I put the final touches on a farewell note to my parents that said little. *I'll be fine, don't worry about me. I've just got to get out on my own.* It didn't sling any blame at them. They were difficult to live with, sure, but they were products of our soul-killing society and burdened with their own problems. Soul killing social conformity held us all in its grip and I needed to escape it before it was too late. They couldn't understand, and how could I explain without being cruel that I rejected everything they held sacred. My running away would hurt them, but I needed to be free from them and, even more so, the stupid, degrading drama of high school. It dragged me down and tried to mold me into a yes-man without imagination, but I knew there was another world out there where I belonged and I needed to find it or die trying.

My note needed a last line to give them hope. *I promise to write you about how I'm doing when I have the chance.* My words sounded stiff, even to me, but I had to keep it short and to the point without revealing my plans and true destination. I slipped the note into the top drawer of my dresser, on top of my underwear. Mom should find it later in the day when she put away my laundry. Then I walked through the kitchen to the side door like on any other day, pretending that everything was normal. But as I stood poised to turn the knob and step out into the larger world, I froze.

Something wasn't right. Dad was usually gone to work by that time, but I heard him talking to Mom in their bedroom off the kitchen. Did they suspect something? I strained to make sense of their muffled words.

"Come on, Joyce, don't be that way. Listen to me, we can work this out."

"Oh, really?" Mom's sarcastic reply sounded slurred. She'd already hit the bottle. "Oh Jimmy, you really think so, huh? Any woman would just love to have a guy like you around the house. So, go to them and get the hell out of here and leave me alone."

Their hushed but intense discussion had more to do with their ongoing marital conflicts than any suspicion of my leaving. Dad seemed to have no clue how to win over Mom. I felt sorry for them both. They were trapped in a pit of quicksand that kept sucking them in deeper and stole the happiness from our family.

I slipped out of the house, carrying only my sack lunch, so as not to arouse suspicion. If they saw me with baggage, they would try to stop me. My schoolbooks were in my locker at school where I'd left them, a burden I no longer needed to bear because I was finished with Fenton high school.

As I cut through the vacant lot next door, I stooped to retrieve my gym bag from the undergrowth where I'd stashed it the night before. The bushy field was all that was left of the extensive prairie that once surrounded our house. It had been a place where the aroma of wild spearmint mingled with the smells of wildflowers and grass, a realm of wonderment to me as a child. I'd often watched pheasants rise, squawking from the tall grass, and seen baby rabbits peek out from shallow burrows. But human growth, *development* Dad called it, was taking the woods out of Wood Dale, which was turning into just another commuter suburb of Chicago.

In 1955, when I was three years old, I watched Dad build our house from the ground up on that flowering lot, but too much had changed over the years. The woods and fields that had been my refuge were replaced by the houses of strangers planted side by side who cared nothing for the natural environment. They screamed at us *damn kids* who cut across their manicured lawns, as we followed ancient paths that had long preceded them, perhaps to as far back as the Potawatomi Indians who'd been driven off to distant reservations in faraway Kansas. Our un-neighborly neighbors preferred isolation to community and remained strangers to each other. Modern communities seemed to be nothing but a series of private families, hermetically sealed off from each other by property lines, as if they were foreign countries to each other.

As if it was any other day, I walked north along Addison Road to the corner gas station where Addison Road ended in a T intersection with Irving Park, a busy, east-west, commuter highway during morning rush hour. This was where I usually caught the school bus, but it was early enough that no one else was waiting there who could see where I went. Without a traffic light or crosswalk, I took my chance and charged across Irving, and hopped over the half-fallen barbed wire fence on the far side, and kept running through the pasture of one of the last working farms in town all the way to the railroad tracks.

Under the tree-shrouded railroad trestle over Salt Creek, I found comfort, surrounded by bushes and whispering willows that hid me from view, and perfumed the air with the scent of spring. I sat on my haunches to catch my breath and listened to the creek gurgling over a line of rocks, where I'd often hopped across from one rock to the other, but the spring showers had raised the water over them. With my back to the busy hubbub of Irving Park, I leaned against the concrete embankment and gazed into the grove of trees to the north. I had far to go, and I needed to stay out of sight from watchful housewives and drivers in the slowly crawling traffic who might be too attentive to whatever they saw along the way. If someone noticed a kid like me who should be at a school bus stop, it could arouse suspicion and they might call the Truancy officers, so I had to be unobtrusive to make it to my destination without getting caught.

The World War Two escape literature I devoured was my survival guide. Only true stories interested me, because I lived in the real world and needed to follow the solid advice of men who managed to get away from prison or concentration camps. Their books recommended patience in making a getaway through enemy country. That's what this once familiar neighborhood was to me: enemy country. I watched television shows, like reruns of *Dragnet* that boasted: "The story you are about to see is true, the names have been changed to protect the innocent."

From all these stories, I knew what to expect. The cops would put out an all-points bulletin for police patrols to search the roads and bus stations for me. In order to not get caught right away, I would have to lie low during daylight and only move at night.

Meanwhile, I needed to get as much rest as I could to help pass the time and keep my anxiety in check. Minutes slipped by. By eight o'clock, I should be boarding my school bus. By nine, there would be roll call in my first class, and I'd be marked tardy. An hour later, I'd be absent from my second class, but as I had occasionally cut these classes, it might take a while for the alarm bells to go off for them to phone my mother. Mom shouldn't find the note I left until the afternoon, but the school might call her first. I felt terrible about the anxiety this would cause her, but I couldn't help it. Regardless of the consequences, I had to get away and remake my life on my own terms before it was too late.

In March I had turned fifteen, the same age my grandfather was when he ran away from home in 1918. Although our situation was different, I seemed to be following in his footsteps. Grandpa was the kindest, most gentle man in my life. As his only grandson, he doted on me, and only he understood something of what I was going through.

He often told me about running away from his adopted parents in Missouri. "They'd a liked to work me to death, keeping me out in the fields all day, plowing them furrows. That's where I learned to handle mules. They was my friends when no one else would so much as give me the time of day. I needed to protect them mules too."

On his journey, he came across a teamster whipping a mule that refused to budge. Grandpa shouted at him, "If I can get it to move, will you stop whipping that poor beast?" He patted and whispered reassuring words and then coaxed it forward.

The boss of the mule team hollered. "You've got yourself a job on this team if you want it, son." And so he made it into the adult world with his first paid job. That long ago time seemed simpler to me than the world I found myself in. It was an era before police radio dispatches, when a big enough boy could find a job alongside men and lawmen had better things to do than hunt runaway teens who hadn't broken any laws. I could only hope for such luck.

As the sun rose, it got hot; I removed the extra clothes I wore and tried to cram them into my already bursting gym bag. The seams of the cheap plastic bag were already starting to fray. I rifled through my gear, weighing the value of each item, and decided that I'd packed too much. I folded my brand-new pair of white pants carefully and left them on the concrete abutment of the trestle, hoping a wandering hobo or someone in need would find them.

Of more importance were a few changes of shirts, socks and underwear, my compact wind-up alarm clock, three pocketknives, ten small cans of Sterno which I'd pilfered from the restaurant I worked at, and more than ten packets of strawberry, vanilla, and chocolate-flavored Carnation Instant Breakfasts. Those items took up a lot of space in my small bag, but as I used up the Sterno cans, I'd have room for the extra clothes I wore. By the second day, I expected to be far enough out to venture into a store for milk to mix with my nourishing Instant Breakfasts. I tried drinking them with cold water, but the powder clumped.

As the morning rush hour died down, I began walking west along the railroad tracks that ran parallel, but a good distance away from the highway and most houses. With careful nonchalance, I strolled out of Wood Dale and through Itasca. My heart raced as I crossed the still busy Route 53, hoping not to arouse the interest of a passing cop I saw. By noon I'd made it through the hamlet of Medina to Roselle, six miles from home. At first, I'd been hidden from a clear view of the road, but at that point, the road angled closer to the railroad tracks, and the trees thinned out, forcing me to walk in plain sight.

Just beyond Roselle, I encountered a blind of poplar saplings to my right, where I decided to stick to my plan and lie low until nightfall. In this little grove of shimmering leaves, I dropped on my belly, pulled out my collapsible binoculars and studied the approaches, low crawling from one vantage point to another within the little green island to make sure that I wasn't being followed.

As time ticked by, waves of panic seized me. *Patience,* I told myself. I had to reassure that part of my mind that wanted to bolt, so I distracted myself by scanning the houses and yards, watching laundry flap in the backyards, a homey sight. There shouldn't be a reason to fear discovery yet. I ate my sack lunch and carefully buried the wrappers to erase any evidence that I'd been there, as my escape books recommended. But I hadn't done enough to be tired, and it was hard to relax and doze through the rest of that long afternoon.

Finally, the distant banging of screen doors and yelling children told me that school was out. By now Mom would have read my note and was probably panicking. I tried not to imagine her crying. It couldn't be helped, and thinking about it would only enflame my sense of guilt and sap my will to persevere. My future was at stake; I had to be free to be me. On the bright side, I was escaping the terrors and bickering of home and school that I knew all too well. My parents would have to forget about me and focus on their own problems.

It was comfortable on the soft grass beneath whispering trees that flickered hypnotically white and green in the gentle breeze, a welcome idyll for my tormented mind. Focusing on happy thoughts, I managed to snooze. Dinnertime came and went. Still, I waited, banishing the gnawing in my belly, as I had so many times before during wrestling training to master my cravings.

My wrestling coach demanded that I fast to compete in a lower weight class, and that gave me practice in controlling my hunger. After some initial stomach rumblings, the pain subsided. It was important for me to think of other things besides food, and I had plenty on my mind.

At dusk, I resumed walking west along the tracks, and found that the moonless night grew much darker than I'd expected. Stumbling over stones and uneven railroad ties frazzled me, and I realized that I should have waited another week, because the twenty-third would be a full moon. Despite my exertion, I was shivering from the cold. Although I'd planned to walk all night, it wasn't even midnight when I stopped at a tiny wooden shack next to the tracks to escape the chill wind.

The shack was only meant to shelter a standing man without enough room to sit, much less lie in the cramped square. I'd rest a few minutes to continue in better shape. Freezing, I put on all my clothes, even pulling all my cotton tee shirts over my long-sleeved shirts for extra warmth. I curled my legs up to my chin on the dirty wooden floor and squeezed my frame against the plank walls.

I remembered hearing about a local boy who ran away only to freeze to death in a barn. Hypothermia, they called it. It was time for me to light one of my Sterno cans, but it gave off a disappointing amount of heat and didn't last long. Trains barreled by only four feet from my ears blasting their horns and shaking the wooden shack right through my body. I couldn't imagine how people living nearby could stand it.

My sleep had to be measured in shivering moments until I finally got back on the tracks, jogging for warmth, and kept stumbling over railroad ties in the dark, but I couldn't give up, I owed it to that dead runaway boy to succeed and prove that there was a chance to escape my tormented life and find a new destiny.

My parents would be frantic by that time, desperate to get me back into that suffocating suburban cocoon. They didn't realize how overwhelmed and trapped they were by their devotion to keeping up the appearance of a "normal" life: the job, the house, the groceries, the cars, and yes, the kids. They had everything but joy, love, and freedom. Nonetheless, the thought of their distress gnawed at me like the recurring complaints of my hungry belly. Imperfect as they were, I loved my parents, but I had to push them out of my mind. There was no guarantee that I'd survive my journey, but I couldn't go on maintaining my sanity at home and school.

My folks had five daughters to raise, all younger than me. As the only boy, I was the odd one out. Losing me would be good for all of them in the long run. My sisters and I had so little in common. Our perspective on life, what interested us, was worlds apart. None of them cared about what was going on in the wider world or read anything beyond what they had to in class. I tried to interest them in critical issues like the Civil Rights struggle or the Vietnam War, to no effect. Their blank faces stared at me; numb to everything I told them. Maybe in a few years we'd be able to understand each other better, and I'd get back in touch.

12

TUESDAY, MAY 16: BARTLETT, ILLINOIS

The sky began to lighten with streaks of red, and I could better make out shapes around me. A small white sign stood beside the tracks. Its black letters spelled out "Bartlett." I'd reached my phase one objective.

Bartlett was only about six miles beyond Roselle, where I'd waited for darkness. This last stretch had taken too long. The railroad tracks curved north toward the larger city of Elgin, and a railroad trestle loomed before me. It appeared ghastly in the eerie pre-dawn light.

This was where I needed to cross the broad Fox River, and I still needed caution. There was a control tower on the trestle. I crouched and scanned the area for signs of guards or workers, unsure if it was manned at this hour or if I'd be visible to whoever was up there. Satisfied that there didn't seem to be anyone around at that hour, I began crossing over the great wooden structure. It didn't have the smooth plank walkway between the tracks like our trestle back in Wood Dale, and I had to be extra careful not to slip between the wide spaced ties and get my foot caught. Reaching the other side, I left the railroad to head south along the river, full of bright confidence that the new day brought me.

People would be waking up to their breakfast and daily routines, and morning traffic increased along the roads. My plan called for me to hide through the day along the Fox River where there should be some concealing woods along the bank, but the area was more urban than I imagined from the maps I'd studied, until I found a small wooded greenbelt, and concealed in the trees was a boy's small clubhouse.

It was only about eight square feet, but sturdily built with scraps of tongue-and-groove lumber, probably purloined from construction sites, as my friends and I had often done to build ours. In curious awe, I entered. There was no furniture on the warped plywood floor. The smell of fresh sawdust mixed with the scents of spring flowers pleased me. Prominently tacked to the far wall was a smiling Playboy centerfold. This shack was a boys' temple to sex, holy pornography. A welcome sight after my long night's ordeal, and I felt assured that the guardian spirits watching over me had led me there.

She was a well-endowed brunette, kneeling sideways, smiling at the camera. Her large breasts poked through an open negligee in a most beguiling way, as if she was inviting me to join her, and I took her for my muse. This shack was the perfect place to wait out daylight. As if in a mystic temple, I forgot my plight as I worshiped at this shrine of lustful desire. Somewhere along the way, I would find a goddess such as this full-bodied woman. The idea quickened my pulse. I should have been exhausted, but under the inspiration of the centerfold, I became pumped full of adrenaline, mixed with lusty testosterone.

After too few sleepless minutes elapsed, I arose, more stimulated than refreshed, and I chanced moving along, rather than wait for darkness. Unfortunately, the shielding trees extended only a short distance down the West Bank of the Fox before I walked through streets that were coming to life with commuters backing out of driveways. Rather than return to hole up in the boy's clubhouse, I decided retracing my steps could appear suspicious to an onlooker, and I hated to retreat. In hindsight, I should have left home on a weekend, when a wandering kid wouldn't be notable.

Forcing a grin, the opposite of how I felt, I whispered, "Get a grip on yourself, man!" To avoid panicking, I had to be my own coach and cheerleader, and it helped firm up my resolve to be as bold as the characters in my books.

The populous city of St. Charles straddled the banks of the Fox River right up to the waterline, and I had to turn away from it. Due west ought to be more open country. In an overgrown weed lot on the edge of town, I forced myself to lie low and wait.

With dusk, I moved on. Except for my stubbed toes, my feet were holding up, and switching my twelve-pound bag from one arm to the other reduced the strain. Alternately, I tucked put it on my shoulder as I forged ahead. It was quite a workout, a good thing I'd gotten myself in shape with track and wrestling over the past year. My Boy Scout backpack would have been ideal, but it could give me away as a boy on a journey, and I didn't want to stand out.

Westward-ho I strode through the farmlands of Kane County, avoiding the small towns of Wasco, Lily Lake, and Virgil. It was twenty-one miles from Bartlett to Virgil, but I slogged even more by staying off the roads and avoiding populated areas. The spring rains had flooded the ground and a succession of barbed wire fences confronted me as I circled around houses. As it grew darker, I blundered into creeks not bridged by the road. Rather than search in vain for a crossing, I waded over, becoming soaked to my knees, which chilled me, adding to my discomfort. It was frustrating reorienting myself in the dark, causing several hours of confusion, convincing me I was off course, moving in a circle. I hunkered down in a depression under a lone tree on bare earth where the cattle had eaten the grass down to the roots.

Shit! The pungent smell of manure assailed my nose. I found myself surrounded by cow patties that I couldn't see in the darkness, but at least I had some protection from the wind in the gully. Getting as comfortable as I could, I took stock of my situation. My clothes were soggy and my shoes squishy from the streams I'd crossed. Wrestling shoes had been a bad choice for footwear. They were designed to reduce friction on a gym mat. A wrestler needed to slide under and around their opponent. The shoes were not meant for traction on rough terrain, but they were the only footwear I'd taken, and already the soles were fraying and coming loose.

My sodden feet were cold and numb. I took off my shoes, rung out my socks, wiped off and massaged my white and wrinkled feet with the extra underwear I carried. Cross-country runs had long ago toughened my feet, but I knew that staying wet spelled trouble. Trench foot, I'd read, was the bane of an infantryman who didn't dry his feet. With relatively dry socks on, I tied the wet ones on the straps of my bag. They would dry eventually, and I'd keep changing them.

Grit and determination were all I had to go on. My flagging spirit demanded I create enough drama, so I imagined myself in a historical scenario. Maybe the wallow I laid in had been pawed out by the buffalo before the white man's cows replaced them. I saw myself out on the frontier prairie, rather than a Twentieth Century cow pasture. Telling myself over and over this was a great adventure made my suffering a little more palatable.

Chilled to the bone, engulfed in another black night, doubt and fear of failure assailed me. What gave me the crazy idea I could make it all the way to New Orleans? How would I make a living when I got there? I'd gambled my very life on this, but there could be no turning back. I opened one of my little Sterno cans and lit the jellied fuel. Its blue flame burned bright and warmed me for a few minutes until it went out. Then I struck another match and lit a second one. By the first faint light of day, I'd used them all. It lightened my load, and I buried the empty cans to hide all traces of my presence.

Hugging myself against the cold, I examined my useless life and all the reasons I had run away. Victory or death were my only option.

13

WEDNESDAY, MAY 17, 1967, OUTSIDE OF VIRGIL, KANE COUNTY

I t had been a particularly long, dark night. Although exhausted, I roused myself with the certainty that it was warmer to move than rest on damp ground. It started out as a repeat of the day before. As I crossed one barbed wire fence and then another, I got warmer, and my teeth stopped chattering. A cold, heavy mist rose over the pastures on either side of me.

When a farmer drove by on his tractor, I dropped into a drainage ditch to avoid being seen, and as I came back up, a large herd of cattle lumbered over to line up along the fence. Their breath rose in clouds as they stared at me with wide-eyed astonishment, and I felt as if these dwellers of the meadow were welcoming me, a fellow creature, in recognition of our kinship.

The countryside was less populated, so I decided to continue walking during daylight, and followed the roads; hoping people would see me as a local kid. By midmorning, I hunkered down in a small woodlot, tucked between tidy fields and farmhouses, where I tried to nap, but I was thirsty and hungry. A quarter of a mile back, I'd seen a little grocery store, so I left my gym bag. The store clerk didn't seem suspicious as he rang up a half gallon carton of milk.

On my way back to the woodlot, an old man pulled over. "Do you need a lift?"

"Sure," I said, thinking it would be more suspicious to refuse him.

"Don't think I've seen you around these parts before, son."

"You haven't. I'm just visiting an aunt for a few days."

"Oh, what's her name?"

He probably knew all the people around there. A wrong name would spell trouble, so, keeping cool, I tossed out a flippant answer.

"I just call her Auntie. I never paid much attention to all that family stuff."

By that time, we'd gone a short distance beyond my little hideaway. It wouldn't do for him to know where I was holed up. "You can let me out right there, on the corner." We were between two houses that sat back away from the road, and I pretended I came from one of them.

"You want me to drop you here? Are you sure?" He seemed genuinely concerned. "Let me take you right up to the house. It's no bother at all."

"Oh, no, thanks." I had to beware of people with good intentions, as well as bad. "Really, I just needed to take a walk and get some exercise." A better idea hit me. "I'm in training for track, you see."

As he drove slowly away, I started walking up one of the driveways, hoping no one was home to ask me about my business, until at long last he got out of sight. I doubled back to the protection of the trees. That had been a close one.

I poured two of my instant breakfasts into the milk carton, shook it up, and drank. It tasted wonderful. The first refreshment, liquid, or otherwise, I'd had since leaving home. My belly was constricted from not eating for so long. I could only drink about half of it before I had my fill. Sleepy, I took a much-needed nap.

An hour later, I popped up like a cork from a deep sleep, and a male voice said, "You'd better go, *pronto, Senior*! They're coming for you now." He sounded Mexican. Somehow, I knew his name was Pancho, and it seemed we'd already been conversing for some time.

"The old man who gave you that ride is on his way back with the cops."

"What about the milkshake?" I said. "My stomach is still full. Should I take it with me?"

"Leave it, Senior, as an offering for the spirits and animals of this sacred place."

My mind was groggy, but I knew he was right. I had to get away from there, but I left the milk carton wide open as an offering. I gripped my bag and slipped out of the woods into broad daylight.

The little used gravel country road wound around a bend. One hundred feet on, I saw a farmer driving a tractor around his field. As I looked at him, my mind cleared enough to wonder who was this phantom Pancho I talked to, and where did he go. I suddenly remembered that Pancho was the sidekick of the Cisco Kid in that 1950s television program I used to watch. He was a character built of my fitful dreams and anxieties, but I hoped he functioned as a sort of spirit guide, a subconscious helper who would lead me to my destiny.

The cheerful farmer waved at me as he drove his tractor on a circuit around his field before he turned his full attention back to his furrows. My mind relaxed, confident I didn't appear out of place. For a moment, I wondered if I should follow the advice given by my dreamland phantom or retrace my steps to my hideout in the woods to get more sleep. I decided I was far enough from home that they wouldn't be on the look-out for me. Phantom or not, Pancho was right. It was time I got started, so I'd follow the road and make better time.

A lightheaded exhilaration overwhelmed me; I felt renewed. That's what a few moments of sleep and a little nourishment could do. In my happy delirium, I began whistling merrily to myself as I made tracks for parts unknown, heading west, into DeKalb County.

14

THE DAIRY KURL

Billboards along my way advertised lavish treats: restaurants and motels with enticing pictures of food for the weary motorist. These images mocked my growing hunger. I felt like an alien isolated from the great American culture that was throbbing all around me, even out in rural Illinois. A series of billboards advertising a Dairy Kurl drive-in appeared every mile or so. Pretty girls smiled at customers from some of them, reminding me that I was alone and friendless in the world. It was three miles ahead, then two, then one.

Maybe a pretty waitress would be awed by my charm. I was no longer a loser, hounded by bullies, but a free spirit, vagabonding across the country, like those carefree guys on the show *Route 66*, driving a sports car from one adventure to the next. Maybe a girl would see in me the hero who could *take her away from all this*. We would charge together into the sunrise, the way it happened in the movies, and I saw no reason it couldn't happen in real life.

There it was at last. The Dairy Kurl was a nondescript drive-in shaded by tall trees with a couple of picnic tables set to one side under an aluminum roof, with a few cars parked in the lot. Despite being trail-worn and grungy, I brimmed with fresh confidence, sure I'd blend right in like a guy coming home from farm work. I set my gym bag down on a table and walked up to the order window. The pretty brunette inside looked a few years older than me. She gave me a brief glance and stood, ready to take my order.

"Gee, what should I get?" I said, hoping to get a conversation started. "Got any recommendations?"

"Whatever you want, Bub, you're the customer." She wasn't taking the bait and called me Bub, of all things, like we were in an old movie. Maybe I'd been transported to a distant time. My reality felt illusive.

"Okay, how about a large cheeseburger, fries, and a strawberry shake."

"Will that be for here or to go?" Her voice was flat, bored.

"I'll eat it right over there," I said, pointing to the table where my gym bag was parked, still hoping that, as she wasn't busy, she might want to stroll over and chat.

"Will that be all?" She finally looked up at me with her big brown eyes. They were lovely dark pools, and even though they were business-like and devoid of curiosity, I could gaze into them for hours. She was not seeing the real me, the adventurer, the guy running off to faraway New Orleans. I longed for her to invite me into her life, if only for a moment, and tried to think of a joke, a line that would ingratiate me with her, something that would make this encounter less fleeting, but my exhausted mind drew a blank.

"Yeah," I said. "That'll do it."

I lingered at the window, toying with the idea of confiding in this alluring girl. What if I told her I was a runaway? No, I could almost see her nose turned up in disgust. This girl probably led a comfortable and predictable life. She didn't long for the privations and uncertainties that came with a hobo's freedom. To her, I was just another flirtatious jerk she had to put up with. It would be better to keep my mouth shut. Somewhere, farther down the road, I'd find the wild nymph I was seeking. Masking my glum feelings, I went back to the picnic table to wait for my order.

Before it came, two young adult couples took the table beside mine. Although they were only in their mid to late twenties, I saw them as middle-aged. But unlike me, they seemed imbued with a smug happiness, free of shivering cold dawns and the terror of being caught and hauled off to reform school. With my back to them, I listened to their banter.

The frizzy-haired girl laughed. "Last night was sure fun, wasn't it? Glad you two invited us over."

The guy with the trim mustache nodded. "We ought to get together again for bridge or poker. Do you play euchre?"

The blond girl at his side tapped his shoulder. "It's much warmer now. We've got this large pool. We've been cleaning it for when it warms up a little more."

"Sure," said the frizzy girl's guy as he pulled her in for a hug and a smooch. "And we've got a grill. We could meet at our place for a barbeque."

I sat across from people who lived on another planet far from mine. They went on and on about how much fun they had together, taking an unpretentious pleasure in the most ordinary things. Even if their domestic tranquility was smug and self-absorbed, I felt a twinge of envy, never having seen such contented joy in the lives of my parents, or even my friend's parents.

Then it occurred to me they were probably childless. At least they never mentioned kids. The thought that such a carefree life ended when people had kids made me sad. No, I refused to accept such an end to joy as inevitable. No matter what happened, I wanted kids someday. The world needs a renewal, and I would break the mold and refuse to turn into a miserable parent.

My angel came out and gave me my order, then turned on her heel and beat it back inside, as if she was afraid of catching something from me. I swallowed my disappointment and munched on my meal. Although I was unused to a full stomach, I needed to eat to keep my strength up, so I kept on munching until finished.

It was time to go. I hoisted my bag and continued west. The food in my belly did wonders, calming my nerves and my optimism rebounded. It had been a trek of about fourteen miles from the hamlet of Virgil where I'd spent the night, and I was only a mile or two outside De Kalb city. A Greyhound bus lurched by. It was time to put myself on wheels.

15

GO GREYHOUND

By mid-afternoon, I reached the bus station. Above the ticket window was a map of the United States, detailing bus routes. If I bought a direct ticket to New Orleans it might raise suspicion. Having watched many episodes of Dragnet, I'd go in stages, because if the police questioned the clerks about suspicious looking kids, my short hauls should throw them off from my final destination. I hoped my nervousness wasn't noticeable as, for the first time in my life; I bought a ticket to a distant city. The balding man behind the counter was so preoccupied with the questions of other customers; he hardly looked at me when I asked for a ticket to Kansas City.

"Do you want a round trip?" His question gave me pause. Getting a round trip could allay suspicions, but I didn't need to waste money on it.

"No, I'm visiting my aunt and she'll bring me back."

The clerk didn't care; he was only doing his job. With a ticket firmly in hand, I felt relief as I dropped into a chair in the empty waiting room. But I was jacked up on adrenaline and could not relax. The minutes ticked by as I fought to stay composed, keeping a wary eye on the glass door and back exit in case any cops came in, looking for runaways.

Eventually, other passengers strolled in to fill seats around me, and I felt less vulnerable. The bus pulled in and I slumped into a more comfortable seat. Any seat, cushioned or otherwise, was a relief after crossing so much of Illinois on foot.

We pulled out, but something seemed wrong. I watched with mounting horror as we circled back to go northeast, along the same road I'd walked into town. We were going the wrong way for Kansas City. Had I somehow gotten on the wrong bus? The bus stopped and stopped again at least twice as I craned my neck, checking for cops summoned to haul me away.

Finally, I realized that we were only picking up packages and a few extra passengers. If I'd only known, I could have caught the bus there. Finally, we turned and headed west, and the miles melted away without effort on my part.

At our first rest stop, late that evening, I got down with the other passengers and approached a long serving line. A boisterous middle-aged woman took my order.

"What'll ya have, honey? Cocoa?"

"The coffee smells good," I said, worried that drinking cocoa would reinforce my image as a kid.

"You want it black, or with cream and sugar?"

"Cream and sugar, please."

Ready filled Styrofoam cups were set out in rows, a line of creamed and one of black, to be picked up as customers moved along the line. I grabbed the biggest size, already filled with a generous helping of cream and sugar. Although I'd had coffee before, for the first time I savored it, achieving a sense of supreme well-being. I'd been alone for so long, freezing and hungry. Although among strangers, I felt a warm sense of community with them. In my mind, I was no longer a mere kid, someone to be pushed around. Adults had rights and privileges, and I seemed to have shed my previous identity among them. I was nobody, just another anonymous passenger as far as they were concerned.

Things were working out. Glowing with contentment, I returned to my seat.

As soon as I got off the bus in Kansas City, I bought another ticket on the next south-bound bus to Little Rock, and when I got there, I bought another one for Monroe, Louisiana. No one seemed suspicious of me. Maybe I didn't have to go all the way to New Orleans.

Through my reading, I'd built up a romantic idea of Louisiana, with a range of opportunities for me to consider in the backcountry. Those boys on *Route 66* were always blowing into small towns where someone would offer them jobs. They entered the life and the loves of the people they met, forging another eventful chapter of their adventure. It could happen to me.

Walking out of the bus station into the bright sunlight of a late afternoon, I found Monroe to be a middle-sized city like any other. Under the hot sun, I stripped off my two extra shirts. They stank of sweat and the smoke of my Sterno cans. This was the south, where I wouldn't need to wear all my clothes or freeze at night. My gym bag's zipper had torn loose and didn't close all the way. One handle was almost ripped off. It was too full. Something had to go. I rolled up my stinky blue polka dotted shirt and stuck it in a hedge as I passed along the sidewalk, but parting with it felt like I was betraying a friend.

Maybe I'd find escapees from a chain gang in the swamps. Who else could I approach without getting turned in? The movies and tales in men's magazines made it seem like the bayous were crawling with outlaws of one sort or another. French speaking Cajuns, swamp people, were supposed to be ruled by their own culture at the edge of conventional law. My information was sketchy, and it was probably exaggerated, but there had to be some truth to it. My blood boiled with excitement at being in this promised land of adventure.

But I'd watched enough tobacco chewing '*good 'ol boys*' portrayed on television shows and the News to have some trepidation about traveling into the heart of Dixieland, where bloody-handed sheriffs, their cheeks swelled with Red Man chewing tobacco, laughed at the camera as they escaped murder charges. The murders attributed to the Ku Klux Klan of *Nigger-loving* whites inspired my caution. As a young fugitive with no experience dealing with adults as peers, I had to be more careful than the guys on Route 66. Somehow, I had to get a job and a place to live, and as an underage kid, I couldn't do it on my own and needed to make friends.

Seeking the wilderness of alligators and outlaws, I reached the south edge of town by sunset and needed a good night's sleep. Under an overpass, I made my lonely hobo camp. It was a warmer night than I'd had in the Illinois pastures. The next morning, however, had a chill to it.

16

FRIDAY, MAY 19, 1967: ALONG THE OUACHITA RIVER

Psyched for the new day, I jumped up off my concrete bed in the predawn light. The mysterious bayous I'd read about ought to be nearby. I began trekking south along State Route 165, ever deeper into Dixieland. The trees shrouding the bends of the Ouachita River were on my right. A railroad embankment ran along my left. From Monroe, it was fourteen miles to Logtown, and another three miles to a place called Bosco.

Bosco? That was the brand of chocolate syrup my grandmother used to buy me. It had a re-usable clown's pointy-head dispenser that screwed on to the jar. You took off the red hat to pour chocolate syrup out of the top. Thinking of my grandparents sent a wave of sadness through me, tempering my joy. They'd be worried sick. When I got settled in somewhere, making money, I'd write and let them know I was alright.

Looking for the bayous, I veered off towards the river on a gravel road that ran parallel to the main drag, but after a mile or two it crossed back to the highway. Expansive white fields spread out to either side of me. It looked like cotton.

Groups of black boys and girls gathered in front of dilapidated shacks, and a sign announced this place as the hamlet of Logtown.

The unpainted general store faced the road and had a tarpaper roof. Unkempt small houses stretched along the side of the road. Groups of black boys and girls gathered in front of dilapidated shacks. They looked like ragamuffins, shabbily dressed in patched and mismatched clothing. It looked more like a plantation scene from an old movie about the antebellum south, rather than modern times. They appeared to be laborers awaiting rides to jobs in the fields. Child labor laws seemed to be flexible in these rural areas.

Although I was a fan of Martin Luther King Jr., against segregation and sympathetic to the growing Black Power Movement, I'd never been in a situation where I was the only white guy and had no experience interacting with Blacks in Chicago, much less the South. All I knew about the reality of what it meant to be Black in America came from television and books, especially *Black Like Me*, by John Howard Griffin. He was a white reporter who darkened his skin to live several weeks as a black man to write about the experience. I worried about how they might see me, and might even assume I was racist, so I had to be careful.

A pickup truck full of similarly dressed youths drove by. They waved and jeered at the others, waiting their turn. A group of about five pre-teen boys and one girl gathered by the store began calling to me.

The girl laughed. "Hey, white boy, where y'all going?"

"Y'all from the North, white boy?" the shortest boy said.

"Oh, he's runnen away," a bigger boy said.

"Yankee boy, you runnen?" the girl said.

They began repeating in singsong: "Yooohooo! White boy's runnen away! Come back here, white boy!" They burst out laughing and other kids, farther along the road, joined in, catcalling and laughing as if this was the most fun they'd have all day.

How did they know I was a Yankee? It must not be the most ordinary thing for a lone white boy to be ambling along this rural road in the land of cotton. These hecklers might blow my cover, and I'd have to run the gauntlet to get away. Although I picked up my pace, I tried to appear calm. If they knew they were getting to me, they would keep it up.

If I asked one of these kids, would he help me? No, I decided. To them, I was just a strange white boy. It had been crazy to get off the bus in Monroe, looking for mythical swamps. A big Continental Trailways bus whooshed by. I needed to be back on board bound to New Orleans. Maybe I could catch the bus in the next town. Leaving the catcalling kids behind, I finally came to a lonely church. Beyond that, a large sign announced the town of Bosco. There was no row of dilapidated shacks and it was nothing like Logtown.

The neat, white painted general store sat on my right, a larger, better kept and more substantial one than Logtown boasted. This hamlet seemed to be composed of just this one large building, although some tin roofs glimmered in the sun farther away across the fields. An old white man was sitting on the veranda of the store with his chair propped back against the wall. He hailed me with a kind voice.

"Y'all just missed the bus, son. Won't be nothing by here for another hour." This old man's affable face and manner were so open and friendly. He seemed to be just making conversation, and there seemed to be no harm in admitting my destination at this point.

I stepped up onto the porch. "Does the bus go all the way to New Orleans?"

"Sho-nuff, that there bus goin ta Nawlens." He drawled his intonation evenly, leaving me unsure if he meant "New Orleans" or some other place called "Nawlens."

I asked again for clarification, but what I got was more of the same. His accent was stronger than the movie actor's drawls I'd heard.

"Where y'all from, boy, up Nawth?"

"Yes, I'm going to see an aunt in New Orleans."

"Well, I'll be," he said in a drawl. "What y'all doing traipsing through this backcountry?"

"Uh..." My mind raced for a logical explanation. "I got tired of riding the bus and thought I'd save some money if I hiked a few miles."

"Reeeeeally?"

"Yeah really. Um, I need to get in shape for track and walked from Monroe."

He leaned forward, planting all four chair legs on the porch. "Mon-row? Didja walk all the way down here from Mon-row?"

"Yep, I sure did. Excuse me a minute." I broke off our conversation to step into the store, where a pretty, dark-haired woman in her twenties stood behind the counter. I bought some oatmeal cookies and a pint of milk. Stepping back outside, I sat on the porch beside the old man, poured one of my instant breakfasts into the carton and shook it up.

The loquacious old man informed me that the owner of the store was also the sheriff.

"That's him ova thea now," he said as a white station wagon pulled up in front of us.

There was nowhere to run, and I swallowed a wave of panic. If I brazened it out, acting naturally, maybe I'd allay suspicion.

The tan uniformed sheriff got out of the car, and I did a double take. He was the spitting image of Andy Griffith of Mayberry USA, right down to his full head of wavy brown hair. Mayberry was a fictional town from anywhere in the south. The show had been on television for years and I marveled at how closely television and movie stereotypes mirrored real life. Or was it the other way around? This sheriff's demeanor was just as cheerful, relaxed, and non-threatening as that television icon. My fear vanished; Andy Griffith was too humane to frighten me. Ignoring me, he waved and exchanged a few pleasantries with the old man before stepping inside to chat with the pretty woman.

"She's the sheriff's wife," the old man said.

Feeling braver, I stepped back inside to do a little people watching. No doubt about it, I was in a mini-Mayberry. It appeared to be a place where people gave each other respect and acceptance. I didn't press my luck, however, and kept a discrete distance.

Some of the black kids who'd jeered me earlier came riding up in the back of pickup trucks. Two of the younger kids stopped in for a coke, and I hoped to God they wouldn't call me a runaway in front of the Sheriff.

Circumstances didn't permit me to pry too deep into the relationships of this community of black and white people. The kids' attitudes were more subdued in there. They wouldn't even make eye-contact with me. It seemed like a segregated society beyond economic interactions. My circumstances didn't permit me to pry too deep into their relationships, but it was clearly different from up north. The kids wouldn't even make eye-contact with me. Back on the porch, the old man nudged me.

"That bus be comen pretty soon, boy. Ya'all betta get up by the road."

It came barreling along, not slowing down as I faced it. The old man yelled at me. "Ya'all betta raise yer hand or sump-tin. Show ya want that ride or he gone!"

The bus was almost abreast of me when I jumped up and down, arms flailing. It took the length of a football field for the bus to screech to a halt and I ran for it. I fumbled nervously for the money the driver demanded. Slowly, he counted out my change and handed me a ticket. Without waiting for me to reach a seat, the bus lurched onto the road and I fell into an open seat in the back as it gained speed, bound for New Orleans at last.

17

ON THE BUS

The faces around me in the back were all black. I wasn't sure if *the blacks to the back of the bus* rule still held in Louisiana. That southern tradition had inspired the Freedom Riders in 1961. Their revolutionary act had merely been to sit together, black and white, in the same section of the bus. Except for two couples in the front seats, I was the only white among black people, and no one seemed to care. On the television news, I'd watched the wild white mobs beating the Freedom Riders and setting the buses on fire, and wondered if times had really changed.

At another rural stop, a young Black man got on. He wore an old jacket that had seen better days, but he had a fancy red hat with a long green feather in it. With an air of supreme confidence, he walked down the aisle and seated himself directly behind me. Across the aisle from him sat a prim, good-looking black woman dressed in gray. Their conversation progressed from an initial glib banter to personal details as they got acquainted.

"I'm a traveling man," he told her. "Being on the road a lot, it's awfully nice to make friends with our people in different cities." He regaled her with descriptions of places near and far.

She nodded politely, and then finally spoke up. "Well, I'm just a small-town schoolteacher." She sounded rueful, with a hint of longing in her voice. "I've never even been out of the state of Louisiana, but I always wanted to travel to the places I've read about."

After some coaxing, he convinced her to let him move next to her, so they needn't shout across the aisle. He waxed philosophically on the distinctions between various parts of *this great country*. "Whites are just out there on their own, always emotionally uptight, with no real community to help them like we Negros have."

The word "Negro" was still in common use, although it was gradually being superseded by Black and Afro-American, with considerable controversy about which term was more appropriate. He began talking about sex, and I listened in attentively.

"We Negroes have a different idea about sex and love from white folks, you see. I been living around those white people for such a long time, both in the North and the South."

"Living down here," she said. "I never had much to do with them."

"Well, their attitudes on both side of that Mason-Dixon line are so different from our Negro people. White men just don't know how to talk to their women. They aren't as comfortable or relaxed as we are. As you know, Negro men and women come together naturally. If we feel attracted, we make no bones about sleeping together. Don't you agree?"

She took a deep breath and straightened up, as if she were about to comment, but restrained herself, so he continued.

"White people are so damn lonely and frustrated. Our people don't get all righteous or possessive about sleeping together. They wallow in all the shame and guilt we do without."

I was intrigued. Nothing else occupied my mind but my own uncertain future. It almost felt like he addressed me, the only white within earshot. My sexual experience was limited to some tongue-to-tongue action in *spin-the-bottle*, but at fifteen, I was as well read about race and sex as I could be. Black Like Me, the book by John Howard Griffin, was my best window on race relations. Griffin, passing as a black man, encountered a sexual double standard. White men wanted sex from black women, segregation be damned, but a black man risked death if he so much as spoke to a white woman. Sex, it seemed, was much more about power and ownership than so-called love. The established social rules, I'd noticed long ago, were not fair or even humane.

Up to that point in my short life, black people hadn't figured into my erotic fantasies. Listening to this traveling man, however, did much to spark my interest. His assertion that a woman could make love to a man of her liking without guilt or shame sounded like a marvelous arrangement, the way it should be. Rather than being a sign of moral weakness and the path to Hell, as indignant bible thumping crusaders proclaimed. A relaxed moral code seemed prone to give people emotional health.

The traveler began whispering lower. "You such a fine-looking woman..." I strained my ears to catch more of his flattering words without success. The pretty teacher giggled with appreciation. I thought that she'd only tolerated and not been interested in him at first, but he'd kept at it, doggedly, until he won her over.

Maybe he was right, and we white people, with our ingrained inhibitions, really didn't know how to win over women. That was depressing. It reminded me of Dad and his sad attempts to win over Mom. Using the stretching of my limbs as an excuse, I kept looking back to check on them and found them inching closer until they were holding hands, then kissing, until she finally snuggled into his embrace.

By the time we rolled into Alexandria, they seemed to have bonded into a couple, young folks in love, or at least a healthy lust. It seemed so right, so natural, and I envied them. I was still the *white man* sitting alone and lonely by the time they left the bus together in Baton Rouge. I also got up to stretch my legs. A Black woman, who had to be at least eighty years old, stood by the row of payphones, looking forlorn.

As I walked up, she reached out to me. "Please sir, could you help me?"

I wasn't used to being called sir with such respectful deference, and felt embarrassed.

"Sir," she repeated. "Where I'm from out in the country, we have party lines and operators put us through. I don't have experience with these newfangled push button payphones. Can you see those numbers? I can't make 'em out." She handed me a wrinkled bit of paper with numbers scrawled on it and put a couple of nickels in the slot before I dialed. An operator came on saying she needed another ten cents. The old lady supplied this. Once we got through, the old lady thanked me profusely before I walked away.

Although I'd done nothing special, that little interchange elated me. It felt good to have any kind of interaction with people, as if I was rejoining the human community.

After a big, creamy cup of coffee and a Snickers bar, I re-boarded the bus, my confidence at an all-time high. The old woman had called me a *sir*, taking me for an adult. It wouldn't be long, and I'd have my feet on the ground, as a *man*, not an unloved kid, in the fabulous city of New Orleans, a place they called the Big Easy. I hoped to God it was true. I'd been a stranger for so long.

18

SATURDAY, MAY 20: HARD KNOCKS IN THE BIG EASY

The bus pulled into New Orleans after midnight, too late for me to explore, even if I had the energy. With only a few snatches of sleep since Monday, I slumped, exhausted, among the assembly of bored, dozing travelers in the waiting room. The inflexible plastic chairs did not recline. People were coming and going, paying no attention to me. This busy place was secure enough for me to lower my guard. With my elbows braced on my knees and my gym bag secured between my legs, I hunched down into an uneasy slumber.

Something awakened me. Through unfocused eyes, my body gripped in the rigidity of sleep, I saw a black man seated on my left. He wore a leather jacket and a red beret that imperfectly hid his mass of frizzy hair, and he was bending overlooking through my gym bag that was clamped between my ankles. My mind was still in dreamland and unable to make sense of what I saw. He turned and looked up into my eyes with a disarming smile as he spoke soothing, melodious words.

"So, you're waking up, my friend? Did you sleep well? We're pals, remember? Let's see what we've got here."

He had to be another helpful dream creature, like Pancho back in

Illinois, and I smiled foolishly at him. In a millisecond, his hand reached deep into my bag and came out with the wallet I'd buried in my underwear. He opened it.

"Hmm, looks nice," he said, pocketing two twenty-dollar bills. "But we'll put this back." He returned a couple of one-dollar bills and pushed the wallet back in before giving my knee a squeeze and rose. "Take care, partner."

Graceful as a gazelle, he crossed the room before my stiff body could unlock and my mind could react to what had happened. A couple of heavyset black women held the door open for him, and without a backward glance, he vanished into the night.

I jolted awake, suddenly remembering who and where I was. This was no dream helper like Pancho. Several older white people sat across from me, staring into space as numb as I must have been staring at the smooth-talking thief. I cried out to them.

"I've just been robbed! Did you see that guy? He took my money."

A middle-aged man responded with supreme logic. "You better call the cops, son, before he gets too far."

An old lady shook her head in disgust. "The cops? They won't be any help at all. They'll only file a report. And by the time they get here, that *darkie* will be long gone. You may just as well go out there and see if you can catch that fellow yourself."

She wasn't serious, but I jumped up in a desperate rage to redeem myself. I'd failed a survival test by watching myself being robbed without lifting a finger, and I was tired of being pushed around and victimized. I'd confront the thief, but I'd have to hurry. My gym bag was still parked under the waiting room chair, its torn zipper imperfectly enclosing my paltry possessions. Besides the fifty dollars secreted in my watch pocket, I still had another wallet stash of money buried in the bag, but I reasoned it would be safer here than with me on the street.

I implored the accidental community sitting around me. "Watch my bag for me, please. I'll be right back!"

A couple of men, slumped next to their wives, nervously returned my eye contact. Because I'd called them all to account, I felt certain they would keep each other honest. Damn it, we travelers ought to look out for each other.

Running to the door, I called to the black women who were starting to leave. "Wait a minute! Where's the guy who just ran out here?"

One blocked my way, saying, "Who you looken for, white boy?"

"The guy who just ran out took my money!"

She backed slowly out of the door, and I followed, unsure if they were bystanders or partners in robbery.

"Okay," she said, suppressing a laugh. "I knows who ya mean. He went that away."

She pointed down the street crowded with partying young black men, dressed in bright clashing colors. They looked like they could all be his friends and partners. It would be crazy to go among them, but half-awake, controlled by irrational emotion as I was, I charged into their midst. The woman shouted after me.

"Watch out, white boy! He a bad one."

The men outnumbered me and I had never fought a serious battle or hurt anyone, but the more I thought about that treacherous, smiling, smooth talking thief, the more pissed off I got, and I fingered a clasp knife in my pocket, a treasured gift from Grandpa. If the thief didn't cough up my money, I'd cut his sneering face. Could I really do that?

The boisterous crowd barely acknowledged me, continuing to clap their hands and snap their fingers, jiving with each other in a playful mood. I hoped that at least one of these faces in the night would have enough honor, or even pity, to help me. They only laughed, mocking me.

"Who took yer money, boy?"

"Where'd the bad man go?"

They pointed at each other, and said, "Was it him?"

"No," the other guy said. "I bet it was him!"

They laughed as they blamed each other and continued their leisurely stroll away from the bus station. I tagged along like flotsam in the tide. Individuals slipped in and out of restaurants or barroom doorways as we progressed up the street, probably looking for pickings as easy as I'd been.

As I turned to one leering, jeering, black faces, he wheeled around and another one spun like a top into my focus. It was like a carnival act. This was the land of Mardi Gras, after all. The pack of artful dodgers danced, joined and separated, keeping me confused and off balance as they became interchangeable, a kaleidoscope of phantom images, their individual features blending before my tired eyes. It was only self-righteous rage that kept me following along in their wake, hoping against reason for a return of my money. My head spun. I couldn't even be sure if the man I sought was among them. A heavyset black woman with monstrous bosoms that heaved mightily as she spoke addressed me.

"I'll help you, white boy! I know the man you mean, an' I hope you get him!"

Her emphatic statement caused a new ripple of laughter from the cavorting crew. Despite the jeering laughter, I desperately wanted to believe this maternal lady would help me. She led me down the street and pointed out one face after another, saying, "He the one!" Then, as that one turned away laughing, she pointed to another, "I mean he da one!"

In sober-faced jest, she kept insisting on her choices. They were all in on this. It was useless and dangerous to stay among them. Hurrying back to the bus station, I found my bag still under the seat. A wave of relief washed over me when I reached in and found the rest of my money intact. In the bathroom, I tucked all the remaining bills into the toes of my shoes, just in case. Back in my uncomfortable chair, I clutched my bag on my lap, trying to forget my humiliation and shame in fitful rest.

19

DRAG TOWN NEW ORLEANS

A nimated conversation buzzed around me as I came to. The faint glow of early morning lit the street outside as it dawned on me where I was. The unwelcome memory of the night before, foolishly smiling at the man who robbed me and, even more foolishly running after him, set me on edge. Stretching my stiff, aching limbs, I sat up straight on the hard seat. I'd arrived at my destination. Next came the difficult part, finding a way to survive on my own. Cramped and irritable, I looked around the bus station waiting room.

Directly across from me sat a delicately thin, decidedly feminine white man. He sat primly on his heels, which were tucked sideways at an impossible angle under his buttocks. Sitting like that must have been painful on these hard plastic seats. He was foppishly dressed in a man's light-colored suit with a pink carnation in the lapel.

I'd never seen an outright homosexual. Gay wasn't a term in use at the time, neither was the concept of being in or out of the closet. Where I came from, boys were always accusing each other of being homos, fags, or queers, which was always denied, not that they had any idea what that meant beyond having effete, female mannerisms.

My friends and I read Playboy Magazine whenever we found an

issue stashed in one of our father's desks or cabinets. The magazine supported the Sexual Revolution in general, and even ran articles about homosexuality. Thus I learned that in most parts of the country, having sex with another man was labeled sodomy, a crime against nature. In some states, sodomy included all sexual activity except vaginal intercourse. That meant oral or anal sex, even between men and women, was illegal whether they were married or not. While I felt absolutely no sexual attraction to men, I didn't hold any hostility to those who did. That was their business, and it wasn't my problem.

Around the man sat a few frumpy, ordinary looking men and fewer women, who seemed to be fans. One normal looking guy in a gray suit spoke with admiration to the thin man.

"I've heard a lot about your act. This time I'm really going to try and catch it."

"Oh, you really must, *dearie*. I'll be performing in town all this week." His hands flitted daintily, preening himself and batting his eyelashes as he talked. "In all modesty, honey, I am the very best and most talented female impersonator you will ever see."

He giggled coquettishly, and then he held his hands up to his face as if pretending to be embarrassed. However, he seemed unashamed of his behavior.

What struck me was how normal the man's admirers seemed. Could they also be homosexuals? Why else would a man be so fascinated by his performance? Where I came from, every mannerism was scrutinized for a fag-like appearance. Almost every guy at Fenton High had been accused of being a fag or queer at some point. All a guy had to do was catch or throw a ball the wrong way, not put enough grip into a handshake, or even glance at his fingernails the *wrong* way, like a girl holding up the back of her hand with her fingers outstretched to admire her nails, rather than the manly way, of looking at his curled fingers, palm up. I'd heard some Greasers brag about beating up queers. Their rage perplexed me, because queers were described as physically weak and non-threatening.

In this crowd, it looked like queer-homosexuals were accepted, but I'd come to New Orleans to be a free man and find real women, not some artificial caricature, and it was too much for me to handle at the time.

In the diner was a convenience store with a large book rack. Prominently displayed on the wall was a large poster in vivid color, advertising a beautiful woman dressed in a sparkling gown. She stood onstage, microphone in hand. Now that's more like it, I thought. Then I read the words underneath the show times.

See the most beautiful boys in female attire. New Orleans most Fabulous Female Impersonators!

Carefully studying the woman, I recognized the thin man. This was his show. How had men come to prefer other men dressed as women, instead of the real thing? The attraction wasn't there for me.

Back in the diner, I devoured an over-easy egg and bacon breakfast with grits, which I discovered to be a bland sort of cornmeal. It needed something, so I poured syrup on it. Then I moseyed through the paperback book racks.

Pimp: The Story of My Life, by Iceberg Slim, caught my eye. Thumbing through it, I caught some titillating, yet troublesome passages. Beautiful, compliant women were depicted as slavishly subservient to this masterful black pimp. He treated them with a superior disdain, and it worked. They worshipped him. The concept both intrigued and rankled me.

I wanted to believe in justice, in fair treatment. I hated this pimp's arrogant enslavement of women, and yet the thought of being in his position aroused me. I assumed that if I were him, I'd be nicer to all the women in my *stable*, as he called his harem of women, instead of treating them as livestock. But the theme of his book was that women, including his beloved mother, fled their nice male protectors for powerful and brutal masters who treated them with distain. The women craved punishment for their love and turned against men who were good to them. This was a puzzling, masochistic behavior that I would come across many times in my life.

Reluctantly, I put the book back on the shelf. I'd have to find a place to stay, a job, and put my life in order, before looking for girls and coming to grips with my own sexual desires.

It was Saturday, so most jobsites wouldn't be open. I'd probably have to wait to find work on Monday, but I couldn't take another night hunched in a chair in the bus station. Turning a corner into the bus station, I found a wall of coin lockers. If only I'd seen them the night before, I wouldn't have been robbed. My aching arms felt relief as I put my broken gym bag in one and strode out into the morning, which was already warming up, and set out to explore the promise of this fabled city.

From the Greyhound Bus station on Loyola Avenue, I found my way to Dauphine and the renowned Bourbon Street. The numerous Jazz, Blues and girlie clubs were either closed or almost deserted at that early hour. Maybe I could get a job as a dishwasher at a club. That was something I had experience with. The barkers sat on tall stools at the door, called out to passing men. "Come on in to see our voluptuous nude girls!" But when I tried to go in, they shooed me away with, "Get lost, kid. Come back in a few years." I needed a go between to vouch for my entry into that adult world.

As expected, the waterfront where I hoped to find a job was deserted behind locked gates on the weekend and a sudden attack of the jitters hit me. I questioned whether I could pass for eighteen, or be chased away from there, too. I needed to find a place where no questions were asked.

My fantasy of becoming a soldier of fortune came back to me. Grandpa joined the Army back in 1920 when he was sixteen and claimed to be eighteen. Our country was fighting a low key war in Vietnam, but wasn't desperate for cannon fodder yet. But I'd read Exodus, by Leon Uris, and it seemed the Israelis were underdogs surrounded by enemies. They had to need men, even green boys like me, to fill their ranks. If I had to, I'd pretend to be a Jew, and maybe they would be more sympathetic to me than a gruff American foreman.

Outside one of the locked gates by the waterfront, I saw a phone booth and checked the dilapidated copy of the Yellow pages.

There was no listing for the Israeli Consulate, so I called information.

The operator's sweet voice said, "I'm sorry, but there is no such consulate in New Orleans."

I had her try Baton Rouge, and she told me that there was nothing in the whole state of Louisiana. "The closest would be the Embassy in Washington DC.," she said.

I swallowed hard to allay my rising panic. In the few hours since I'd arrived, I found no prospects, and I needed something right away before my cash wasted away. Although I knew becoming a soldier of fortune was a long shot, a rising desperation began to take hold of me.

I trudged back to the bus station and bought a one-way ticket to Washington, DC, which took most of my remaining money. Then, since I was leaving town, I bought a postcard and addressed it to my folks in Wood Dale. *I'm all right*, I told them. *Don't worry about me.* Letting them know I'd gotten there was my new deception plan to misdirect the pursuit before I left the city. The next bus to Washington, DC, didn't leave until later in the day, which gave me enough time for one more stroll around the French Quarter before I left this city of impossible dreams.

20

CHANGE OF FORTUNE

On my way back to the bus station from Bourbon Street, I cut through a park to Canal Street. A tall man with a prominent paunch, dressed in baggy, gray clothing, called out to me.

"Hey, boy, where're you off to in such a hurry?"

He looked like a hobo; his gray stubble matched his thinning hair. After six days of hard travel, I probably looked rough too, but without the stubble. He was about my grandfather's age and his rolling gait and friendly voice reminded me of him, so I waited for him to catch up.

"I'm Tom Smith," he said, extending his leathery hand.

Smith was a popular pseudonym, and I wondered if it was his real name. I shook his hand and gave him my own more creative *nom de guerre*.

"I'm Jim Hassle, pleased to meet you."

"You know, Jim, I have a job. Now I'm trying to find me place to live and start fresh. How are you fixed for that?"

I told him that I'd just come into town, and also needed a place, as well as a job. I didn't tell him I was an underage runaway, but he might have guessed it.

"We ought to partner up," he said, nodding his head. "I don't just want a place to flop, you see, but a nice place where I can feel at home." He gave me a wink. "Where we can bring a woman once we get settled in."

"Yeah," I said, trying to contain my enthusiasm. "That's what I'm looking for, too."

It seemed that my guardian angels were looking after me. Tom was the first human being who had taken an interest in me since I hit town. He knew of a place where I could find work, and there would be no embarrassing questions about my age, and I would get paid at the end of each day. It looked like Tom was the mentor I needed to navigate the adult world, and I decided to trust him.

He extended his hand again and said, "Partners?"

"Okay, Tom, we're partners." And we shook on it.

Things were looking up; my emotions had gone from hasty panic to sublime confidence. Too bad I'd mailed that postcard to my parents, but this was a big city, and I reassured myself that the police probably had other things to do than chase down an out-of-state runaway. We walked back to the bus station where I got a full refund for my ticket to DC. What a relief to have that money in my pocket again.

It was a hot afternoon, and I was soon dripping with sweat as Tom and I walked up Canal Street, a broad avenue graced by a pleasant, green meridian. We turned right on Rampart Street, that ran northeast along the edge of the French Quarter to where it intersects with Toulouse and there we saw a sign. Tom pointed to it and shouted in triumph. "Well, looky there, Jim."

Alamo Hotel
clean, quiet
daily rate $2.50 and up
Inquire about our weekly rates.

"Let's try that, Jim. Weekly rates, huh? On the outside, this place looks a damn sight better than some of the fleabag hotels I've been in."

We walked up the steep steps into the open front hall. The first door on the right was marked MANAGER. We knocked and waited, then knocked some more, before we heard a thump and a scramble of hurried movement within, followed by whispers, before a woman shouted. "Just a minute! Be right there!" A few more minutes ticked by before a youngish man's face appeared at the crack of the door, with the security chain still on.

"Yeah, can I help you?"

Tom smiled. "We want to look at a room."

"Just wait here." The man called over his shoulder. "Honey-pie, get me my pants."

He closed the door to take off the chain and reopened it fully. A sweaty, strawberry blond woman came up behind him, barefoot, with a white sheet imperfectly wrapped around her curvaceous form.

"They just want a room is all," he said, turning back to us. "Just wait a moment." He closed the door on us again, leaving Tom and I waiting in the hall, presumably while he got fully dressed.

Tom nudged me in the ribs. "Did you get a look at her?" He whispered too loud. "She's a fine looken woman. Ain't she? They's fucken in there!"

That sounded coarse and embarrassing, yet it excited me. I took a deep breath to keep from blushing. Indeed, I had seen her. She exuded an erotic charm that went far beyond the airbrushed Playboy centerfolds I was used to drooling over. She was no paper doll, but a real life, flesh and blood woman. Although she was no teenager, I didn't care; I was not in high school anymore. That miserable, unsatisfying life was behind me at last. In my new adult life, I likely wouldn't find a girl my own age, and I was more than willing to try my luck with older women.

The door opened, and she let us in. "He'll be right with you," she said, straightening her disheveled hair. "He should've let you wait inside, for goodness' sake."

As she let us in, I noticed that in her hurried dressing, she hadn't pulled up the shoulder strap of her shift. It drooped down her arm, provocatively exposing the rounded top of her fleshy bosom almost to the nipple. Her flushed skin was damp with perspiration, alluring to my hungry gaze. I politely pretended not to notice, but to be indifferent to the charms of this voluptuous angel would have meant that I was beyond feeling. Quite the contrary, I indulged in fantasy about her.

Maybe, I wondered with earnest hope, this hotel was a bordello, like I'd read about in old New Orleans. Inexperienced kid that I was, how did I know what to look for? I'd keep my mouth shut and let Tom do all the talking.

We followed the manager upstairs to a one-room apartment, much bigger than I expected.

Tom whispered to me. "This is obviously no flea bag hotel, Jim."

The one large room could be partitioned by a folding screen, creating two sleeping rooms. There was one double bed, but the manager got an extra folding cot from a storeroom. The kitchen was ample for us, with a gas stove and refrigerator. A screened porch lay off the kitchen's back door. A few trees reached up to us from the yard below. With the breeze, it was a cool and shady place to hang out.

"Where's the toilet?" Tom said.

"It's in the hall. You'll have to share it with the other tenants on the floor." It consisted of only a commode and a sink. "If you want a bath or a shower, you'll have to go to the larger bathroom farther down."

"What if it's busy?" I said.

"You can use one on the other floors. That's the way these old buildings are in the Quarter."

"Alright," said Tom. "What are your weekly rates?"

"It's fifteen dollars a week."

The toilet and bathroom down the hall was a minor inconvenience, but at fifteen dollars a week, it was all I could afford. After getting robbed, I had about a hundred dollars left and needed to stretch my money, but with Tom paying his half share and his promise of a job, I could build up my savings and be on my way to making ends meet. Then I could look for a girlfriend, or two, or maybe even three.

The manager cleared his throat, looking a little sheepish before continuing. "I'll have to insist on two week's rent paid in advance. That's thirty bucks."

Tom pulled me aside, a concerned washing across his face. "You see, Jim, I'm flat broke right now, but Monday is my payday. I'll give you my share then, I promise."

What else could I do? I'd come a long, hard way and, being friendless, had to trust my new partner, so I paid the man. Tom wouldn't turn me in as a runaway if he depended on me for a share of the rent. The manager left, and we settled in. My travel-worn gym bag was about shot. The packets of instant breakfast took up space I could have used for more clothing, but I'd made it, and things were looking up. Once I was in the dough, I'd get a better one.

After plopping my stuff in a drawer, I walked down the hall and took a much-needed shower under the too short, antique showerhead, while standing in a century old ornate tub. Then I put on the cleanest duds I had, those I'd washed out most recently in a Greyhound sink. Tom only had one pair of baggy pants to change into. Freshened up and hungry, we ventured out to explore our new neighborhood on the edge of the French Quarter.

Tom grabbed my shoulder, "I'll only shop at mom-and-pop stores, ya know. Those big supermarkets are running all the little shops out of business, busting up the neighborhoods."

I hadn't expected such a strong anti-corporate feeling from a down on his luck bum. Tom rambled on.

"Family run stores give a neighborhood its character, you see. Supermarkets are destroying the whole goddamn country."

We were in luck. We found a little place nearby, run by an old couple, and Tom made small talk with them. He was a personable, well-spoken man, much like my Missouri born grandpa. His accent and word choice sounded just like him, too. Thinking of Grandpa saddened me. I loved that old man, but I was doing exactly what he had done at my age. He'd understand, aside from his racism, we were much alike.

Tom, I concluded, was heaven sent to me. Someone might have called the police on me if I'd spent another night in the bus station. Sleeping on the streets was out of the question; I'd get arrested for sure. As for joining the Israeli army, that, I realized, was a crazy, impossible idea. Desperation had hijacked my common sense.

Tom turned to me. "Jim, we need to get us some fixin's for the next couple days."

There was a small freezer section. My idea of nourishing comfort food was chicken potpies. I chose some for our dinner, along with eggs and bacon for breakfast.

Tom picked up a six-pack. "Jim, we need to celebrate our partnership. I don't drink nothing but Pabst Blue Ribbon if I can help it. That okay with you?"

"Suits me just fine."

Although tempted to save cash, having arrived at my destination after a tough journey, I needed to relax and celebrate my newfound freedom. I was throwing my fortune in with Tom, placing my faith in providence. It was a gamble, sure, but that's what made my new life a real adventure.

Tom looked me up and down with pursed lips. "You damn well need some new shoes, boy!"

After slogging miles through woods and marshes, my wrestling shoes were coming apart. They hadn't been designed for the abuse I'd put them through. Tom found a pair of blue canvas shoes that had a hard tan plastic sole.

"Down here everybody wears crepe shoes," he told me.

"What?" I wasn't sure if I heard him right. "You mean crepe, as in crepe paper? That's what I used for art projects in kindergarten." That didn't sound sturdy.

"Don't you northern boys wear crepe shoes?"

"Never heard of it. Except for the brown sole, they look like blue canvas tennis shoes to me."

They were comfortable, and on sale for four bucks, so I bought them. Things were looking up. I did a quick accounting. The six-pack of beer was a dollar. A dozen eggs, bacon and a loaf of bread came to a buck and a half. What money I had left would have to last until I found a job and got paid, but the doubts that had assailed me earlier in the day were gone. I was setting up house as a free man.

We popped the pies into the oven and the beers into the freezer to chill. When the timer went off, we took our supper out on our veranda, as Tom called our second-story porch, relaxing in the cool evening breeze. The weather in Dixie was as hot as I'd expected, at least in the daytime. From time to time, we'd pull out another cold beer.

"Now this is living!" I said as I sipped another Pabst with Tom. After traveling so far alone and suspicious of everyone I met, it was nice to have a sympathetic pal like Tom to talk to.

"Tom, I'm itching to get a job before these expenses tap me out."

"It's the weekend, Jim! Don't worry, I told you Monday is a sure thing. All you gotta do is be there early, before sun-up, to get picked for a crew. You'll get paid at the end of the day. I'll pay you my share then, too. Everything's gonna be just fine and dandy."

Just fine and dandy; that was another expression my grandfather used.

After gulping down my last Pabst, I was content to retire for the night. It had been a long day, a longer week, and a hellacious journey. I hadn't slept in a bed since leaving home on Monday. Tom was an old man, so I let him take the larger bed. As it was still hot, we stripped down to our skivvies under a sheet, all that either of us required, but Tom warned me that I should keep my blankets handy.

"It will get damn cold by morning, Jim." And sure enough, it did.

With foresight, Tom had placed an old coffee can he found between the stove and the latched screen door to the porch. The can proved useful. It beat running down the hall to the toilet every time we had to pee out our beer in the middle of the night. From my side of the divided room, I tiptoed past Tom, fast asleep, to the kitchen. Without bothering to turn on the light, I aimed at the can, which my night vision could barely make out.

Shooting from a standing, or rather a swaying, position, it's a wonder that I hit the thing at all. I tried to redirect my aim by the sound of the spray hitting the can but kept overshooting to the wall until I finally heard the ringing of the can telling me I was on target. Most of it got in the can. The mess on the floor wasn't too bad. In the morning, I'd have to clean it up.

21

SUNDAY, MAY 21: A DAY OF LEISURE

Dim sunlight began poking around the curtains to light up the room when Tom sat up in bed. "Jesus Christ, Jim. I went to take a piss and found a hell of a mess in the kitchen."

"Yeah, I missed, sorry Tom. I'll clean it up first thing."

I went out in the hall for the mop and bucket. By the time I got back, Tom was already frying the eggs and bacon we'd bought the night before. The piss can was almost full, as Tom had put in his full share. We probably needed a bigger can if we drank beer every night.

"How did you make such a mess, Jim?"

When I explained, he laughed. "Well, of course you missed, boy! You can't hit the can from a standing position. You got to pick it up like this here." He put down the spatula and picked up the can in both hands to demonstrate. I took it to the toilet in the hall to dump.

"Make sure to rinse it out really good, Jim, so the edges are clean enough to hold tonight." He divided the bacon and eggs onto two plates. "Now let's eat, Jim. I'm hungry enough to eat a mule!"

"Tom, let's go where we can meet some girls today," I said, pushing away my empty plate.

Tom laughed and slapped his knee. "On a Sunday? You want to go find 'em in church?" He rubbed his chin stubble. "We ought to go to the big park on Lake Pontchartrain. Maybe we could get lucky there. There's a real nice zoo and everything. Some girls are sure to be there."

First, I needed to do my laundry. I only had two pairs of pants, including the one I was wearing. They still bore the grime of my trek through the Illinois swamps. Tom had nothing more than the clothes on his back, but they were cleaner than mine. The rest, he said, were being kept for him somewhere. He'd fetch them on Monday.

The residential part of the quarter breathed of its French and Spanish history. Due to the tropical climate, a strange musty odor of decay hung in the air, mixed with the scent of blooming flowers. I associated this with its earthy reputation. Many scandals, crimes, and bold adventures were launched from these precincts over the centuries by unscrupulous men who meddled in governments all over Latin America.

The Laundromat was within the French Quarter, a block or two behind the Alamo Hotel. It was a funky old place, with the familiar smells of damp fabric, detergent, and bleach. Only a couple of old crones were in evidence that morning. I dumped my unsorted load in the washer and bought a small box of soap powder from the vending machine to cut the past week's crud. While waiting for my wash cycle to end, a woman came in.

She was no crone, but no raving beauty either, and went straight to the pay phone beside me and dialed. She spoke French into the receiver; her singsong accent fired my interest. My ruminations about the ghosts of French Louisiana seemed to have taken physical shape in the frail, almost anemic, young thing with straggly hair. After she hung up, I tried making small talk.

"You have a nice accent. Are you Cajun?"

"Oh, no," she said, laughing. "I know nothing of Cajun. Though, I am from France, visiting a relative here. I have been here only one week."

"Me too. I just got in yesterday. Maybe we could explore this town together sometime."

She flushed red and turned away. "No, that would be impossible. I am not alone; I have family. They will take me around." Then she hurried out the door without a wave goodbye.

Perhaps I appeared less of an adult than I liked to think. The girl had several years on me, probably in her late teens. I was willing to overlook that detail, but she was too much like a scared puppy, a mere wallflower of a girl. I was on the lookout for bold and adventurous women. They had to be out there somewhere. I wanted an alluring, flirtatious fox of a woman with an insatiable sex drive, like I'd been reading about. It was so hard to sit tight and wait patiently for my destiny to unfold.

Tom and I caught the St. Charles streetcar to West End Park, situated on the shores of Lake Pontchartrain. He beamed at me and said, "This is the oldest working trolley in the world."

The trolley ride, my first, reminded me of Rice-A-Roni commercials, featuring a happy streetcar ride that I'd watched for years. The jingle went: *Ding-ding, Rice-A-Roni, the San Francisco treat!* This trolley had reversible wooden seats, so you could change direction from back to face forward or, like Tom and I did, flip one side to talk face-to-face.

The Amusement Park was crowded. All the girls I saw were with someone, and I envied the guys with dates to squire around. Tom soon plopped down on a bench. "Go ahead," he said, winking at me just like Grandpa used to. "Maybe you'll find some little honey to hang onto and, who knows, maybe she has an older aunt who might like to meet me."

Grotesquely smiling giant heads rotated above the haunted house. That could have been fun, but I saved my dwindling dough and skipped the paid attractions. I bought a bottle of pop and walked around the zoo, watching people watching the animals. A raucous group of about ten white, college-aged boys came charging up to where I stood by the monkey cages.

They began throwing peanuts with force, trying more to hit the poor monkeys than to feed them. "Hey, you ugly, stupid beast, catch this!"

They laughed and jeered at the animals when they scored a hit, or the monkeys flinched. The boys had strong southern accents and wore pricy, casual attire. They were probably fraternity students from a nearby university. I was as tall, but not half as burly as they were. These boys foamed at the mouth when they got to the large ape cages.

"Here you are, you fat lipped nigger! See that? Ha, I got him in the face! See that? He's too dumb to duck! Stupid nigger-ape."

Although I'd heard it said many times before, the vehemence with which they spit out the "N" word shocked me. It peppered every slur they came up with.

The apes, which until then had been docile, cringed and then screeched back at them. With futile desperation, they charged at the bars, unable to reach their tormentors, who continued trying to hit them with peanuts. Every movement the apes made, no matter how ordinary, was interpreted by these southern lads, as to how stupid they were. The boys exemplified a visceral hatred that both terrified and angered me. Images of lynch mobs came to mind. I'd seen the same mocking faces on bullies in my high school and on television, as white mobs attacked Civil Rights marchers. At least the apes were in cages, protected from serious harm.

Evolution classed humans and apes as near relatives. Whether they believed in evolution or not, the boys had no love for their animal kin. They showed an arrogant contempt for 'lesser beings' locked up and on display for their amusement. By extension, their slurs denigrated black human beings, equating them with this sub-human order, and their own ancient roots on the evolutionary tree, but as I was a white human, they ignored me. Mothers with children in tow gave these louts a wide berth.

A phrase I remembered reading popped into my head. "The flower of Southern chivalry" lauded the gallant lads who died for the Confederacy in the Civil War. They may have been boys like these, spoiled brats, used to raising hell and getting their way. But like the other spectators, I didn't stand up for the apes. Maybe if I wasn't a runaway, I would tell those boys a thing or two.

22

MONDAY, MAY 22: WORKING

y wind-up alarm clock exploded at five in the morning. It was still dark outside, and the chilly, foggy-damp air knifed into me when I jumped up and dressed in my two long-sleeved shirts, while wishing I had a warm coat. I didn't expect the mornings to get so cold in Louisiana, when the days were so sweltering.

Tom yawned. "No time for breakfast this morning, Jim. It's over a mile away and you got to be in front of the line early to get hired."

We took a brisk walk over to Canal, then along Tchoupitoulas Street until we came to number 620, a shuttered building between Lafayette and Girod. The sign above the garage door read "Roberson Advertising Service." Ten unshaven, rumpled men already stood in line outside the door.

"Get in line with them," Tom said. "You'll be all right now. I'll see ya tonight." He took off for his own job, wherever that was.

All I could do was wait and shiver, as more men, most of them wearing jackets, straggled up behind me. As a Northerner, I ought to be used to this cold, but I wished I'd carried a warm jacket to the balmy south.

One of the older, white-haired men nudged me. "You never get used to it, son." He wore a heavy, hooded parka that looked brand new and didn't shiver at all. "I've lived around here for many a year, young man, and I still find it a rough *row to hoe* getting up every morning."

Finally, another old man, helped by a woman who was probably his wife, walked along the line with a tray of Styrofoam cups filled with steaming coffee, for which he charged an outrageous fifty cents a cup. All they had left were black and un-sugared, but I sprang for one, and it warmed my hands as I sipped. Even a moderate rise in temperature was welcome.

It seemed forever before the wide doors opened and we were allowed inside the dusty garage that reeked of diesel oil from the military style cargo trucks that were parked inside. The men referred to them as deuce and a half, two and a half ton trucks.

The dispatcher stepped out of his heated office, ceramic coffee cup in hand, and I felt a warm draft. He obviously ran the show and had organized the day's assignments. His receding gray hair was slicked back. That, with his bulbous nose and commanding presence, made him the spitting image of LBJ, our President Lynden Baines Johnson. He even talked with that same Texas drawl. I almost expected him to come out with a classic line like *mah fellow Amuricans*. Instead, he passed out assignments to the drivers, who stood to one side.

Tom had prepared me for what to say when he came to me. "I never worked here before and need to fill out a W-2 form."

LBJ eyed me suspiciously. "What's your age, son?"

"Eighteen."

"Good, that's what you'll put down on the form. We're almost ready to move out, so fill this out and join the line behind a truck."

A weight lifted off my back. No, he didn't seem to care if I was an underage runaway or an escaped felon. That wasn't his problem. I wrote down my alias, Jim Hassle, then a social security number, which I made up off the top of my head and put down no dependents.

The men formed up in crews, and the drivers counted them as

they climbed up into the backs of their trucks. Those with preferred work partners boarded together. As I wondered which truck to go to, someone called out. "Hey, boy, over here!"

I looked up to see a younger man with no gray in his black hair beckon to me. "Are you in a crew yet?" I shook my head no, and he waved me aboard.

As I climbed in, someone shouted from the back. "Hey, kid, come back here and sit with me!" He extended his hand. "I'm Johnny Marino."

I caught myself before I blurted out my real name. "I'm ah, Jim, Jim Hassle."

"Put 'er there, Jim." We shook hands. "You and me are going to be partners and I'm gonna call you Jimbo. That's what I called a past partner of mine. I can read people, Jimbo, so I can tell that we'll make a good team working together."

I was flustered by all this sudden attention. The guy who first invited me in had a sour, disgusted look on his face, as if he'd been scooped, or maybe he was just tired of Johnny's non-stop chatter.

Johnny ignored him, grabbed my shoulder, and kept talking. "You see, Jimbo, partners is much tighter than just friends. We got to watch out for each other. I'll show you the ropes and you and I will make some good dough today."

As we bumped and swayed along the highway, most of Johnny's words were lost in the roaring of the truck. His accent combined with the gush of his words was hard for me to follow.

That almost put me off.

The guy who first called me into the truck leaned forward and shouted over the engine to me. "Sometimes I just want to tell that son-of-a-bitch to kiss my ass! Don't you?"

I gave him a weak smile, not sure what to say. He was right, but I needed all the friends I could get. At least I was no longer alone in the swamps of Illinois.

We were crammed side by side along the benches lining three sides of the jouncing, swaying truck. Stacks of bound paper filled the middle of the truck bed and functioned as our temporary footrests.

At one point, Johnny lifted the edge of the canvas tarp behind us and shouted. "There it is!" We were on a great bridge over a vast stretch of awe-inspiring water.

"That's the mighty Mississippi," Johnny said. "On the other side is Jefferson Parish, where we'll work today. It's the best place to do this kind of job, gets us out of the concrete jungle."

Soon we were rolling through middle-class neighborhoods of manicured lawns, sidewalks and tidy brick and tile homes, our target area for the day.

Men were let out of the truck in pairs every few blocks. Each work team was handed a couple of canvas pouches filled with stacks of flyers. They advertised all manner of household merchandise, meat, milk, and other produce on sale by local merchants. The driver wrote down how many stacks he gave to each, along with packets of rubber-bands. The men needed to keep track of the number of stacks they passed out. The tally at the end of the day meant money.

It was our turn to go. Johnny and I jumped down and were handed two full bags. After shouting a few directions at Johnny, the truck shifted into gear and was gone. We were suddenly alone in the welcome quiet. Looping the single strap over his shoulder, Johnny gave me the lowdown. We would be responsible for putting the papers on all the doorknobs over several blocks.

"We'll start in the middle of the block, and each go around in opposite directions and then cross the street to the next block, splitting it between us. I call this crossing our T's. If you see a flyer already in place, you'll know I've gotten there ahead of you."

He demonstrated his technique on the first three houses. Grabbing a set of papers with one hand while opening and readying a rubber band with the other, he single-handedly rolled the paper into a tube and slipped the rubber band around it while approaching a house at full gallop.

"We've got to move fast to make the dough. And it helps to be ambidextrous." He looped the rubber band over a doorknob or some ornamental ironwork on the porch and kept moving onward to the next house as he lectured me.

"Speed up, but stay on the walks. The residents complain, so we aren't supposed to cut across the lawns. Watch out for the truck, too. The driver will come swinging by to check on us. He's our overseer, making sure we do this goddamn job right."

Johnny hardly took a breath as he rattled on, and I had all I could do to keep up and absorb his wisdom as I jogged after him.

"We get paid a few cents for each advertisement we pass out. The more we distribute, the more we earn. Some guys try to dump their stacks in the bushes, but the driver checks on us. If houses have been skipped, he'll notice." He looked at me sharply. "You ready? Start here, you're on your own. See you at the end of our run."

It sounded easy, but I wasn't at my best. Despite having run cross-country track and wrestling, I became winded too soon. Maybe the hard journey down had taken too much out of me. Or maybe I needed time to adjust to the below sea level altitude and extremes of the climate. Skipping breakfast sure didn't help. I'd already come down hard from my coffee high, which left my brain in a fog, but I couldn't disappoint Johnny, and with my belly growling, I stumbled along as best I could.

Not all the streets conformed to a neat grid pattern. There were dead ends and cul-de-sacs that required creativity to cover. I wasn't ambidextrous and too easily confused. At times I got turned around or forgot which side of the street I'd already done. A couple of times, I had to retrace my steps to be sure of where I was and where to go from there. It was more than I could do to keep up.

Johnny was in his mid to late twenties. It galled me to be a healthy teenager, and stumble around in his dust like an old man. Johnny began covering my area until I caught up, which meant that he was passing more paper than me. At last I caught up, finding him sitting on the lush grass of a vacant lot, waiting for me. I finished my side and flopped down next to him, grateful for a breather.

"Looks like you're all done in, Jimbo! You're moving like one of those winos I've been stuck with." He laughed. "Ok, I'm kidding. You'll catch on. All you need is time."

Discouraged as I was, I hoped he was right.

"Well, we've reached the end of this run. We have to wait for the driver to swing back, so we may as well rest up. We're finishing up a neighborhood that was left-over from last week and then he'll take us to another route," he said.

Johnny began playing with something on the ground.

"What's that, Johnny?"

"Don't ya have Doodlebugs up north?"

"Never heard of 'em."

They were long, many-legged bugs with strips of armor on their backs. When he poked them, they rolled up into a tight armored ball, reminding me of an armadillo. Then he rolled them around like marbles on the ground. That occupied us for a few minutes. It was peaceful out at the edge of town, and I was drowsy.

Johnny stretched to his feet. "Well, it isn't noon yet. We won't make much money if the driver don't show up soon, but we might as well have us an early lunch. I know this area. Follow me."

We followed a path through thick woods and came to a tavern and a little country store on the other side. I grabbed a pint of chocolate milk and a berry pie while Johnny got something I hadn't seen before.

"You ain't never seen a Moon Pie, Jimbo? Must not have 'em up north. That's where you're from, ain't it?" He laughed good-naturedly. "You got yourself a Midwestern accent, Jimbo."

I thought I'd one-up him. "You sound like you're from New York."

He laughed. "I'm from right here. Funny thing about a New Orleans accent, it don't exactly sound southern. I reckon we owe it to all the Boston ships that docked here over the centuries. We leave off the r's. So, iron is *ion*. We say *wata* for water, just like New England."

We sat out in the sunshine. Famished, I wolfed down my pie.

"We need us a little liquid refreshment," Johnny said. "Don't worry; the driver will wait for us."

We went from the bright Louisiana sunshine to a table in the dark gloom of the tavern. There were only a couple of old men standing belly up to the bar, chatting with the barkeep. Johnny took my shoulder. "Act naturally," he whispered. "Let me handle this and everything will be all right." That implied that he knew I was under eighteen.

The bartender called out to us. "What'll ya have?"

"A couple bottles of Dixie, if you please." Johnny turned to me and said, "That's the beer of choice in these here parts."

The bartender promptly brought over two cold bottles of Dixie and set them on the table before us. Afraid to give myself away, I didn't look up at his face, and tippled my drink as suave as I could, playing the part of an adult. It seemed to work. The bartender went back to his conversation at the bar, and I relaxed.

The cold beer was refreshing. Johnny winked at me and with a big grin said, "I'll speak plainly, Jimbo, because we're partners. I'll bet you still haven't busted your cherry yet. Have you?" I felt myself blush crimson. He slapped me on the back. "Yeah, I'm right, aren't I, Jimbo? Don't worry, I get it. We just have got to get you laid. Don't we?" He clinked his bottle against mine. "Let's drink to it!"

He'd read the deepest strata of my mind, which gave me a mixture of embarrassment and relief, but I needed to confide in him, man to man, so he could help steer me into the adult world and unlock my future.

"Sure, Johnny, you got me. I've never had sex. Do you know any women I could meet?"

He took a swig of Dixie while he seemed to weigh his words. "Well, there is this sweet little barefoot girl. That's what I call her. She works behind the bar, but strange to say, she don't wear no shoes at work. Man, is she built! I'll introduce her to ya soon enough. She's a wild one, so I expect you got as much chance as me to make it with her."

Broadening our conversation, I told him about my roommate, Tom, and our Alamo hotel.

"Tom? You mean old Tom Smith?"

"That's what he told me his name was."

"Look, Jimbo, we're partners now and have to look out for each other. So, I'm giving it to you straight." He squinted, making a serious face. "I worked with that old man. We're all down on our luck, sure, but that Tom is just a no-good lush, a useless drunk. He'll take you for all you're worth if you don't get the hell away from him."

That sounded too harsh on old Tom. Although I'd only known him two days, I felt he'd saved me, and we shared a bond. Johnny had to be exaggerating. Tom was supposed to give me my money that night after work, and I didn't want to believe otherwise.

"I'm no lush," Johnny said. "Sure, I had a rough patch a while back, like most of us on this job, but I'm in control of my life now." A look of regret darkened his features. "I used to be a pilot. Flew into Crescent City. Know where that is?"

"No."

"When you see New Orleans from the sky, it looks just like a big Crescent in a bend of the Mississippi, so us pilots call it Crescent City. Yeah, I fucken blew it, lost my flying license and the woman of my dreams. Startin' over now, but I got a new hustle going on that I'll tell you about later. Don't worry; I'll bring you into it when I think you're ready."

He faced the bar. "Let's have another round of Dixie here, bartender!"

This time, the bartender shook his head. "You can have a beer, but not the kid."

Johnny shot me a sly, knowing wink. "This is my partner! He's eighteen, fully a man!"

"Shit, that kid don't look eighteen to me. Ya gotta show me some proof or I can't serve him. I don't want no trouble in here, ya know. He got one beer already. Count yourself lucky."

As we walked out, Johnny yelled over his back, "I ain't drinking here anymore without you serving my partner too!" Outside, he said to me, "You got to bluff and stick to your guns, Jimbo, but always leave yourself a way out. This is Louisiana, after all. We've got the most liberal drinking age laws in the country. They need to sell their beer and will usually only question your age after the first or second round."

Johnny didn't seem to be worried about being charged with

contributing to the delinquency of a minor. Such things seemed irrelevant in Louisiana.

On the way back along the wooded path, we ran into a couple of towheaded kids, playing in a shallow creek. A girl of about four looked after a toddler boy. They pointed their sticks at us.

"Stick 'em up!" We raised our hands in surrender as they grilled us. "What'cha all do'en out here anyways? Where ya'all from?"

Johnny was grinning from ear to ear. "Listen to them talk, will ya? I bet'cha never heard anybody say 'ya'all' up north, did ya?"

"We've got a fair number of hillbillies up in Chicago, ya know." I thought of my classmate Eugene, the first guy who ever pulled a knife on me, back in third grade. That was a hell of a thing for a best friend to do, when all I said was that I didn't believe one of his wild stories.

We made sure the kids knew where their home was and waved goodbye. When we got back, we found the truck driver finishing his sack lunch in the shade of his cab.

"Hey Johnny, I figured you was at the bar back there. You men are just in time for me to take you to our next area."

The relaxation, food, and especially the beer and companionship, had nourished my body and soul and helped me finish that Monday better than the way it started. Coming back across the Mississippi, Johnny began trying to convince me to move into his hotel.

"My place ain't fancy, Jimbo, but it's cheap as dirt and you'll save your dough. What more do you need than a place to flop?" I remained noncommittal, so he kept after me. "If you lived by me, you'd be closer to work. I live on Girod, right around the corner from Tchoupitoulas Street, half a block from the St. Charles streetcar, too. Stop in when we get back."

I said I'd think about it. Catching the rolling eyes and insider winks from his compatriots, I wondered how much of what he said was true and if Johnny was to be trusted any more than Tom.

The foremen tallied up each of our flyer output and handed it to LBJ, who poured over the results in his office. Finally, he began calling out names and passed out small manila envelopes with cash inside.

"Hassle!"

"Here!" Opening it, I found six dollars and fifty cents. Johnny got double what I did, as he'd helped me cover the ground I'd missed.

"Don't be discouraged, Jimbo. You'll do better tomorrow. We're working a new territory. Stick with me, and things'll look up."

I walked with Johnny up Girod to see where his place was. True, it would be a convenient location, much closer to work. I was beat and still had a full mile to walk back to the Alamo.

"I'll think about it, Johnny. I ought to get back and talk to Tom about my money first."

"No problem," Johnny said with a dismissive wave. "If not tonight, I'll see you tomorrow. Be an early bird and we'll make some real dough."

23

A CHANGE OF ADDRESS

My mind was in a whirl about what to do. I'd arrived friendless in New Orleans. Suddenly, I had two partners and a job. Johnny was trying to steer me away from Tom, and Tom, who had been my first friend and made my whole New Orleans adventure possible, had the voice and mannerisms of my grandfather. The younger Johnny seemed more capable of introducing me to women and the adventurous side of this fabled city, and his place was a lot closer to work.

I bounded back up to the Alamo Hotel, eager to share my feelings with Tom. When I reached the manager's door, left open for the breeze, he called out.

"You don't need to pick up the key; your pal is already upstairs." There was a strange inflection in his voice, something he wasn't telling me.

Upstairs, I found our apartment door open too. I burst across the threshold and stopped just in time. The floor was covered in a slimy, purple-green sheen of vomit. It reeked of booze mixed with stomach acid, worse than the smell of kid's puke I'd come across in grade school. Scattered here and there in the liquid were chunks of solid food. Worried about getting it on my new shoes, I stepped around the safe edge of the room to see Tom. Wearing only his pants; he was lying sprawled across the bed. His arms outstretched like Christ on a cross, dead drunk. An empty bottle had rolled into a corner, and a huge Jalapeño pepper caught my eye. It appeared he had swallowed it whole, un-chewed, before he upchucked it.

What a homecoming! It was all I could do to keep my lunch down as I surveyed the scene. All I wanted was to get out of there. Johnny was right, Tom was a drunken bum. He should have had the decency to wait until I'd come home and paid me before going on a bender. Getting my money was uppermost in my mind. I hoped he hadn't drunk up his whole paycheck.

To approach him, I'd have to mop the floor, and then I could search his pockets. Mastering my nausea, I got the mop and bucket and went to work. Johnny's warning rang in my head as I mopped. Tom would ruin me, even if he didn't intend to, and I had to think for myself. If he had my share of the rent and food, he'd be worth a chance. If not, it was *adios*.

As I finished, Tom rolled over and began singing out of tune. His face came alive, showing various expressions as he mumbled in his dreams. Transfixed, I leaned on the mop handle and watched his antics, as he began pleading his case to a dream woman who was probably long gone from his life.

"Oh sugar, Maggie! I didn't mean nothing by it, honest. Maggie, please don't go. God, I love you baby, honest I do."

Although I felt sorry for him, I couldn't let sentiment cloud my thinking. With the floor passable, I approached the bed and reached into his pocket. He grunted and jerked away, rolling into his wallet. Tom had survival instincts. I didn't really want to pick his pocket and decided I would let him prove he was true to his word.

"Tom!" He sat up, blinking, rubbing his eyes with his fists, and said, "Jim, you're home! How'd the job go?"

I came right to the point. "Did you get paid, Tom?"

He reached into his pocket and pulled out a big wad of cash with a fifty-dollar bill on top. There could have been over a hundred in there. He looked at it with wide-eyed surprise, like he didn't believe it, and held it tight in both hands, as if afraid I'd grab it, and I almost did. As I leaned in, Tom lurched away and fell face down on the bed.

"Just give me what you owe, Tom."

He only grunted in reply. I didn't have the heart to wrestle it out of his grip and decided to wait until he sobered up. Even after mopping the floor, the nauseating smell lingered, and I wanted to get the hell out of there. Maybe I should check out Johnny's place and come back to deal with Tom later. I threw my clothes together, wrapping them up in the clean sheet from my bed.

"Are you going to the Laundromat, Jim?" He didn't wait for me to answer. "Would you wash my pants too?"

They had been hit by a stream of his vomit, but he carefully rolled them up and handed them to me while still gripping his wad of cash. I didn't have the heart to say no, although I hadn't planned on trudging to the Laundromat, but as I waited for the washer to finish, I went over the events of the day and made my decision. To hell with Tom. I was too exhausted to make another round trip back to him after seeing Johnny's place, so I'd deal with him later. After I crossed Canal Street, I didn't look back, dissolving my partnership with the old man. Let him enjoy this cozy apartment, paid up for the week. It more than repaid him for helping me get on my feet.

Johnny was hanging out with a couple of the guys in front of his hotel and called out as I approached. "Jimbo! I'm glad you made it." He gestured to a man with a serious face. "This is Frank, our esteemed manager. He is the gatekeeper to this domain."

Frank nodded and checked me out with a wary eye. Black-haired thirty-something, he stood behind a half open Dutch door to the right of the entry. The closed bottom half of the door held a shelf where he collected rent and noted the payments in a big ledger, like St. Peter at the pearly gates. Everyone had to pass him before he let them in. With a dry, deadpan voice, this sober, pinch-faced manager intoned the rules.

"A room is a buck and a half a day, paid every day as soon as you get back from work. Got it? I don't brook no nonsense from anyone.

No pay, no stay. Understood?" His patience had long ago worn thin dealing with deadbeats, which most his roomers undoubtedly were.

Johnny tried to soften him up. "Aw, come on, Frank. Haven't I always paid on time?"

Frank didn't crack a smile. "I'll have to check my books on that." He Drilled me with cold eyes. "Another thing: we didn't allow any women inside. Don't try to tell me she's your sister or mother, either. I have enough trouble without all that complication."

Johnny nudged me, his back to the manager. "Don't let that bother you, Jimbo. We'll get around it somehow," he whispered.

Johnny left me in Frank's humorless care to go on a tour of the place. He led me into an almost palatial foyer, through a set of double doors along a wide, worn carpet, and up a short flight of stairs. Beyond the wide imposing entry, this place was dilapidated. It had once been a grand mansion with large rooms and vaulted ceilings. The original rooms were divided into small cubicles, with jerry-rigged partitions that didn't extend all the way to the ceiling. An enterprising thief could hoist himself up and over the partition if it was worth his while to do so. Even Frank remarked on that, saying he took no responsibility for lost or stolen articles.

The closet sized room he showed me was a ramshackle affair, with peeling paint. There was no comparison to my apartment at the Alamo Hotel. The single bed took up half the space. A beat-up dresser with four drawers and a desk lamp was the only other furniture. Doubt flickered across my mind. Maybe I should forget this and go back to Tom at the Alamo. But I'd done enough trekking across town for one day and decided to stay, at least for one night. It would be a new adventure.

Frank continued our tour. Some residents didn't even have the privacy of a room. Across the hall, almost right outside my door, a frail old white-haired man lay on a bed next to a louvered window, open for the occasional breeze. He was wracked by long rasping spells of coughing. There were a few more beds, some of them occupied, farther along the hall.

"This is the best we can do for this poor fellow," Frank said, evidencing more concern than I expected. "He's bedridden and dying, you see. He can't afford no hospital, has no family who wants him back. His luck has run out." Addressing the old man, he asked, "Feeling any better today, Pops?"

The old man grunted and resumed coughing, and Frank shook his head and clicked his tongue in pity.

"Sometimes he's like that, but I guess we'll all grow old and die someday. Won't we?"

I considered myself a compassionate guy. It shouldn't bother me to have the poor old guy out there. I didn't expect to be doing more than coming in late and sleeping there. This place was good enough for now.

"The toilets are down the hall." Frank pointed the direction with a wave of his hand. Like the Alamo, this building had probably been built before anybody had indoor plumbing. The broken and rarely cleaned toilet seats and leaking faucets were of a much lower standard than the Alamo. I saw no tub or shower and needed one after getting hot and sweaty in the sweltering climate.

"How is a guy to wash up?" I said.

"Showers are out in the backyard. Follow me. This damp climate produces too much humidity, so it's better to keep them outside."

We went out a back door into an unroofed courtyard littered with junk. Old boxes, flattened beer cans and empty bottles sat in crates. Moldy wooden slats were scattered around the yard to walk on, giving some protection for your feet from the even muddier, moss-covered ground. Colorful tiles poked out of the mud in places, making me wonder how it must have looked a century ago. Like everything else, the plumbing was jerry-rigged and leaky.

Along the outside wall of the building stood a row of three dilapidated stalls with mildew-covered plastic curtains. None of them were clean, but one stall was in worse shape than the others, with a broken showerhead that dripped a steady stream of rusty water onto a layer of mud that covered the cracked and sinking tile floor. There was only a partial roof over another stall and no roof at all over the third. No roof only meant that rain could add some fresh water to your showering and kept the yard a slimy bog. The half-clogged drains were overtaxed.

Gesturing at the stalls, Frank said, "I recommend that you wear shower shoes in there. The one on the end has the better working water line."

My worn-out wrestling would have sufficed for shower shoes. Unfortunately, I had left them at the Alamo. Unappealing as it was, taking a shower was the first thing on my agenda. If only I'd checked this place out before going to the Alamo, but I was too tired to trudge back, so I paid Frank his buck fifty to stay the night.

The water standing in the pipes was lukewarm, but then suddenly spouted cold, as unheated fresh water came out. That was a refreshing shock! It was just like camping, and I'd done a lot of that. After I dried off with the towel I'd taken from the Alamo, I slipped into my new crepe shoes and gingerly stepped back over the slimy ground to my room and took stock of my new abode.

The Alamo was a rundown hotel, but compared to the Girod Street flop house, it was high class. Girod Street was located in the middle of Skid Row, inhabited by hopeless down-and-outers, and I'd become one of them. Edgy as it was, this place fit in with what I'd read about the New Orleans of a century ago, when brawling river men made do with wretched lodgings on the edge of proper society so they could spend their cash in the bawdyhouses. It seemed like I was in a time warp from an earlier century, but I'd made my escape from suburbia and would thrive somehow.

If I saved my money, I'd get a better deal. Like Johnny said, he had on the other side of this sprawling complex. He told me he had a real room, not a cubicle, but he paid twice as much as I did.

The combination lock from my high school gym locker only secured the flimsy door from a lazy thief. Alone in my new refuge, I flopped on the narrow cot to take stock of my new surroundings. I'd leave nothing out to interest a thief, certainly nothing worth climbing over the wall for. I was in a hole, but at least I was free of the horrors of the hypocritical, bully-ridden fishbowl that was Fenton High. No matter how terrible things got, I was making my own way.

The space at the top of my partition allowed in some outside light, but with the table lamp turned off, it got dark at night. Sleep embraced me for a while, and then the dying man's hacking cough awakened me.

Hagh, ugh, rah-ughah! Throughout the night he interrupted my sleep, wheezing, coughing up phlegm that he spit into a can. Poor guy, my ass! My pity wore thin. It was irritating to have a noisy dying man right outside my door.

24

TUESDAY, MAY 23: YODELING IN THE CANYON

Although I wasn't crazy about the Girod Hotel, I wouldn't have to wake up so early to get to work. Johnny treated me to breakfast at the only nearby diner open at that ungodly hour. We gobbled down a large stack of pancakes, bacon, and hot coffee before standing in the work line. A good breakfast made all the difference in my attitude, and it turned out to be a longer workday than Monday had been. I earned eleven bucks, though the more experienced Johnny always outdid me. He insisted that I hadn't hit my stride.

After work, I intended to see Tom at the Alamo. He ought to be sober enough to cough up what he owed me, and I'd bring him his freshly laundered pants, which I hoped he'd figured out how to get around without. It served him right, getting all liquored up before buying a second pair.

Johnny slapped my shoulder. "Forget about that old man, Jimbo! Tonight, I want to fill you in on some things. I plan on making you my partner in the hustle I'm working on. I'm a dealer, you see. We're going to make some real money and move up in the world."

That's all it took to dissuade me from the trek across town. Johnny and I got to know each other's stories. Johnny rambled on non-stop, but most of his barrage of words went over my head, and I got tired of asking him to repeat things unless it seemed important. I didn't tell him my real name, but finally admitted to being a runaway.

"I figured as much," he said. "No big deal. You're tall enough and look like a guy with a head on his shoulders. You'll make it okay if you stick by me." Then he launched into another chapter of the saga of his life.

"I used to be an airline pilot, Jimbo, been all around this big 'ol world too. I've seen some amazing things, things I wouldn't believe if I hadn't seen 'em with my own eyes. You see, Jimbo, I haven't always been a bum and I sure as hell won't remain one long. I just need a decent break, same as you."

Johnny took me to his favorite place for dinner. The Camp-Inn Restaurant and Bar was at 801 Camp Street, on the corner of Julia Street. The name on that street sign inspired Johnny to reminisce about a former girlfriend named Julia.

"Man, could she fuck! We'd go all night long. I'm serious, Jimbo. The worst mistake of my life was losing her. After that, I kind of took what we pilots call a death spiral. I lost all direction. It was suicide in slow motion, but hey, I'm rolling with the punches now. There's plenty of other fish in the sea. Right?"

He pushed the menu across the table to me. "The best deal at the Camp-Inn is the pizza."

We washed it down with a pitcher of Dixie beer for thirty cents. Johnny was a regular, so no one thought to card me. That was another reason the Camp Inn became our favorite hangout. Boisterous, grandiose Johnny was a character straight from one of the men's magazines I'd devoured back home. He was surer than Tom to usher me into the adventurous life I craved. I felt like an emancipated man on the rebound.

Although Johnny kept mentioning his hustle, how it would make him rich someday, he remained mum on the details. "I'll let you in on it soon enough, Jimbo. Be patient, you'll get a piece of the action too." Then he changed the subject. "God, I love New Orleans. Can't think of any city I'd rather be. Wait 'till you see

Marti Gras. That's one hell of a party and the women go fucking wild."

Marti Gras was over eight months away. I hoped I didn't have to wait that long for some action. After a big cheap meal at the Camp-Inn, we walked to a local skid row bar for a couple more Dixies. Johnny leaned back in his chair and rolled out long and instructive monologues on everything under the sun, especially sex.

"Did you know that Chinese women's cunts go sideways? They're slanted like their eyes. Like this..." He illustrated by wagging his finger right to left. "They're not shaped like a round-eyed white woman's that goes like this." He wagged his finger forward and back.

"Aw, come on, Johnny, you're pulling my leg."

"Well, I'm the authority on that, Jimbo. Did you ever see a Chinese gal's slit?"

He had me there. My experience was limited to a couple of girls my own age and race. We played doctor until we were in Junior High. Their silky-smooth pubic hair had just begun to grow out when they suddenly stopped our co-ed fun.

"Okay, Johnny, prove it by introducing me to some Asian women."

Johnny broke out laughing and slapped his knee. "You crack me up, Jimbo. You're right though, we need to get you laid." He winked. "Me too, man. It's been a coon's age. I'm going through a hell of a dry spell. We've got to get us more money first. Ain't nothing free in this world, Jimbo, especially love."

Though I suspected he made that up about Asian vaginas, it took me a few years to prove him wrong by my own exploration of that netherworld region of Asia. But Johnny's tales were as entertaining as they were instructive. He schooled me on how to satisfy a woman, a topic left out of my high school sex-ed class.

"You've got to learn how to eat bearded clams, Jimbo. Know what I mean?"

"We don't eat a lot of clams in the Midwest, but I read that they're aphrodisiacs."

Johnny burst out laughing again. "They're not the clams in the ocean, man! It's what a woman has between her legs, unless, of course, she shaves her pussy. Get it, the beard?

The women's pubic area had been airbrushed out in the men's magazines I had seen up to that point in my life. That was the trend in photography until much later, although I had glimpsed some girls my age, whose pussies were covered in fine hairy, almost transparent gloss.

Johnny continued his sex-ed class. "You got to stimulate a woman's clit using your tongue like this." He modeled this for me by wriggling his tongue rapidly between the "V" sign of his first two fingers. "We also call it yodeling in the canyon."

Picturing a yodeling Swiss mountaineer at this job cracked me up. Johnny both scandalized and tantalized me with his graphic depictions of cunnilingus. It sounded disgusting the first time I'd heard about *eating out* a girl from my older schoolmates. Johnny made it sound palatable, sexy, maybe even delicious.

"It's quite a skill, Jimbo. Women crave sex just like a man once they've been done good and proper. Most men only think about their own satisfaction, shooting off as quickly as they can. They never even guess their woman has needs, too, but turnabout is fair play. The more excited a woman is, the more it excites me and the better it feels when I explode like the Fourth of July fireworks.

He took another sip of beer. "No kidding. Sex can be so much better than the *slam-bam* most people put up with. It's a skill and an art. You ever hear about a trip around the world?"

"You mean you took a trip around the world?"

"No, not that. Your body is your world. She'll take you on a special trip around your body like you haven't known before. It's something offered in the higher-class cathouses I've been to. I spent a lot of great times in them, here and overseas too. They take good care of you in some of the high-class joints in Thailand." He leaned his chair back against the wall, and his eyes rolled up into his head as he channeled the experience to me.

"She'll bathe you good and proper first, then dry you off with a big smile on her face and have you lie on the bed. Then she, and maybe her friend too, if you get two girls. By the way, that's what I recommend. Having two girls make love to you at the same time is the best experience you will ever know. They'll start flicking their tongues all over you. They'll ignore your cock at first, go all around it though. Starting from your toes, licking between each one, and then slowly moving up your legs, to your belly and chest, even nuzzling into your armpits, which sends a wild thrill through me." He took another sip of beer and leaned back again.

"They'll turn you over and play with your ass. Believe me, women love a good hard butt, like yours, and you will love the sensation as she plays with it. There's a lot of erogenous zones there that will keep you hard and randy. Only then will they turn you over to focus on your hard cock. It's service with a smile, Jimbo!"

"Johnny, the waiting is making me crazy! When will I get my chance?"

"Don't rush things, Jimbo, have patience. Good things come to him who waits."

Johnny almost sounded like my dad when he said that.

25

AN EVENING IN PORT

After a couple of days in my new place, I finally went back to the Alamo to check on Tom. I'd never have made it without his help. I would have arrived broke and friendless in Washington DC., where I was sure to find nothing but handcuffs and a forced return to Illinois.

By then, I knew I should have waited until Tom sobered up and got my money before I left. He owed me money, but I owed him for my making it in this city. Listening to Tom's drunken delirium that day, begging a long-gone dream woman to take him back, made me feel sorry for the poor old sot. He couldn't help it. Life hadn't treated him fairly, and maybe I hadn't either, disappearing like I did. But at least I'd left him with a studio apartment, paid-up for the week, and it was time to collect.

The Alamo manager looked surprised to see me when I knocked on his door.

"Is Tom Smith in?"

He scratched his head. "Gee, he took off the day after you did. I'm busy cleaning up the place for a new tenant. You guys left it a mess and won't get your deposit back. Come on up and take a look if you want."

I hadn't expected Tom to be gone already. He had a fistful of cash that should have helped him rebound, unless he drank it up and blew the job that he'd told me about. Maybe he was counting on me to hold the place together so he could continue to drink himself into oblivion. Too bad, I liked Tom, if only he didn't drink up his money. I wondered where he had gone to. Maybe he'd gotten picked up by the cops, and might be sleeping it off in the drunk tank, while I camped in a jerry-rigged room with walls that didn't reach the ceiling. We'd both wasted the comfort and security the Alamo offered.

The manager led me upstairs to the room where I found a large aluminum garbage can, filled to the brim with our discarded belongings, trash now. It sat on the back porch where Tom and I had our first meal together. It made me sad, remembering the joy and promise the place held for me. My worn-out wrestling shoes and unused packets of Instant Breakfast sat forlorn on top of the refuse. The packets had weighed me down over those hard-traveled miles across Illinois, only to lay uneaten in a filthy can. I was tempted to grab them, but held back. The manager droned on about how he had to clean the place.

"There was slimy vomit all over the floor..."

That surprised me; I had cleaned up Tom's puke before I left, so he must have gotten drunk and thrown up again after I left. It was almost impossible to keep an alcoholic, like my own dear mother, from drinking. I should have stayed the rest of my paid week, gotten what Tom owed me, and tried to help him get control of himself. It was in the past now. I had to stay focused on my current situation.

Johnny was the new partner I placed my faith in. Things could only get better. We'd be rolling in the dough before long. I just had to be patient.

We got off work early on a particularly hot and sweaty day that sapped your willpower away, and both of us were bushed. Frank wasn't standing at his door to take our rent door as usual. A guy who looked to be in his early twenties stood there. He was more cheerful than crabby Frank and cracked jokes about him as we placed our money on the counter.

"Hello gentlemen," he said with a wink and a smile. "You seem to be enjoying the sunshine today. Lucky you don't have Frank's sunny disposition to heat up the day even more."

Johnny laughed. "That Frank is such a goddamn skinflint. I always make sure what I pay gets jotted down in the ledger."

The other guy shook his head. "Oh, he's honest enough, but he wouldn't let you get by owing him a dime, or even a nickel! Don't worry, see here?" He pointed to the ledger. "I've got both of you down as paid for today."

Johnny clapped my shoulder. "Jimbo, it's such a goddamn hot day. Let's hang out at my place, save some of our hard-earned money. It's cheaper to drink at home and I want to catch up on my writing. Did I tell you I was writing a book?"

This was the first time I'd heard about it, but I might have missed it in his rapid-fire yakking at me.

"Someday you too ought to write a book, Jimbo."

"Nah, I got nothing to write about yet. No one wants to read about some goddamn kid like me, running away from all the comforts of home to live with a bunch of bums."

Johnny chuckled. "Who are you calling a bum, anyway? Going through a rough patch, hitting a low point, why it's all part of the crazy experiences you live through that gives your life meaning. More so than some pampered rich boy who hasn't been tested, who doesn't have the range of experience to know what it's all about. Get it? That is what makes a story interesting to me, Jimbo."

"Well, Johnny, I bet your book will be a best-seller for sure, full of wild sexual adventures, and you've had your share of ups and downs."

"I hope so, but I've got to get it polished up and published first. Come on, let's go to my place."

Johnny's room was on the backside of the rambling Girod Hotel. We climbed to a rickety wooden causeway, with clapboard rooms along the side. His room was far nicer than my hole; therefore, it cost twice as much. Its walls went all the way to the ceiling. He even had a screen door to let in the breeze behind a double locked secure door to keep out thieves. It would never be featured in Home and Gardens magazine, but Johnny had given it a personal touch that my four walls and a bed lacked. Besides a bed, the furniture consisted of a comfortable swivel chair, a messy desk and a couple of filing cabinets overflowing with books and maps. The reams of paper stacked in boxes must be drafts of his manuscripts. He was working on something, but said he wasn't ready to show me yet.

"Go ahead and make yourself comfortable, Jimbo."

I sat on his bed while he leaned forward in his chair and fumbled through a cluttered stack of paperback books, found what he sought, and tossed it over to me.

"Here's the book I've been telling you about, Jimbo. It'll help you understand how this *ol* world of ours *really* works!"

The dog-eared paperback was The Had, by Richard Gehman. Johnny had been plugging this book as a work of profound insight into the human condition since I'd met him, but with fabulous New Orleans under my feet, I wasn't in the mood to curl up with a book. But it was so damn hot outside. My lust to get out and experience life would have to wait another day.

From the title, I guessed what the book was about. Being 'had' meant getting tricked, taken advantage of in some way. In a sexual connotation, a guy could say that he'd *had* a woman if he'd screwed her. I wondered if Johnny's enthusiasm about this book had to do with seeing himself as a man of the world, a survivor of the vicissitudes of life who lived by his wits. He'd been *had* by our screwed-up rat race of a society.

Johnny opened a little cupboard in his desk and pulled out a bottle and a couple of tall glasses, and started to pour. "*Did'ja* ever drink port, Jimbo?"

"Is it some kind of wine?"

"It's fortified wine that gives you a jolt. Good tasting too. Here you go Jimbo, have a snort!" He handed me a half full glass and went back to scribbling at his desk.

It was tasty, alright. Kicking back, I sipped and read while Johnny wrote. Gulping strong wine probably wasn't the best way to appraise the merits of The Had. It featured some guy with a negative attitude, bitching about his life and what a loser he was. By the third chapter, I still had no interest in where it was going. I skipped ahead, but the guy still couldn't find any joy or enough chutzpah to plunge into life and find the solution to his trouble. The character seemed too much like the people I'd come from. There were too many more exciting things on my mind, but as a favor to Johnny, I kept reading.

Johnny held up the bottle. "Have another?" I polished off my glass, and he refilled it. It seemed important for me to keep pace with Johnny, and I soon lost track of the number of refills.

Eventually I'd had it with the book, but Johnny had been lavishing so much praise on it that I couldn't tell him it stunk. There had to be something to this book I wasn't getting. Then, without warning, it hit me.

I felt woozy and when I stood up, the room spun around, so I sat back down. "Man, this shit snuck up on me, Johnny!"

We hadn't eaten after work, expecting to go back out when it cooled off, and I had too much wine on an empty stomach.

"Are you okay?" Johnny's voice was full of concern.

"I feel like throwing up."

"You'd better go to the can, or back to your room. We'll call it a night."

That was a wise suggestion. The memory of what damage Tom had done to our place at the Alamo was fresh in my mind. I made it through the screen door and lurched on my way, but I managed to make a couple of wrong turns in the labyrinth of the hotel before I homed in on the dying man's coughing. That got me safely back to my room without spilling my guts. After fumbling with my combination lock, I latched the door behind me with the hook and eye nail. Without undressing or pulling back the covers, I collapsed face down on the bed.

A drunken slumber overwhelmed me despite the noises from the old man outside my door. Tonight, I thought, he shouldn't interrupt my sleep.

Suddenly I woke, convulsing with nausea. Weak as an infant, I couldn't make it to the door. The contents of my stomach erupted like lava from a volcano. I barely had time to hang my head over the side against the wall before a great purple stream spewed forth, missing the bed, but painting a garish color on the wall below it. My second and third eruption went better, getting most of it on the floor. Being drunk was no fun. All I wanted was sleep and to be sober again. Completely spent by the effort, I sank back into a dreamless sleep.

Wham-wham-wham! The pounding on my door wrenched me out of unconsciousness. I wondered if it was a cop, and almost didn't care. What right did a cop have to bother me, a grown man making a living on my own?

"Hassle! Open up, I know you're in there! Come on now, you chiseler, pay up! Open this door or I'll smash it in!" He sounded like Frank, the manager, and I couldn't understand why he was so pissed off.

Without even trying to raise my head, I shouted back. "I paid already! Check the damn book." Groggy as I was, there was still no question in my mind that I was within my rights. That son-of-a-bitch, Frank, must have known I was drunk and was trying to con me.

"No, you haven't, Hassle! I've been here all afternoon. You slipped past me somehow."

"I paid the other guy. You weren't there. Go ask Johnny."

"Open up or I'm getting the cops."

That was all I needed. "Just hold your horses!" I stumbled to the dresser, flicking on the lamp. The room was spinning around as I dumped my pocket change on top of the dresser. My eyes couldn't focus as I tried to count it out. All the while, the manager kept shouting and banging on the door, telling me to hurry up. To shut him up, I unlatched the door and fell back on the bed.

"There, count it out yourself and leave me alone!" I was too sick to care if he took it all. My paper money was still tucked away in my watch pocket, like Grandpa taught me. Only a couple of dollars in change was at stake on the dresser, so he couldn't clean me out.

Frank stood open-mouthed, shocked at my condition, and his

voice softened. "I just want the buck fifty that you owe me and nothing more."

He poked through my jumble of coins, as if afraid to catch something. I watched him through slit eyes. My mind was clear, but my body was almost useless. After he counted and recounted the coins several times, he was satisfied he had the right amount. Now that he had what he'd come for, he spoke gently.

"Hassle, you better put your money away and lock this door again." He waited to walk away until I got up to latch the door. That was decent of him, as if he weren't trying to burn me for extra rent.

I'd barely sunk back into deathlike slumber before his heavy fist pounded the door again. *Wham-wham!* "Hassle, open the door!"

I let him back in. He looked sheepish. "I'm sorry. It was my mistake. You paid all right, just like you said. I didn't expect that you'd come back so early before my shift." He handed me back my assortment of nickels and dimes. "This was just an honest mistake. You'd better count it because I don't want to cheat you."

With my eyes still unable to focus, I tossed it all back onto the dresser in a show of contemptuous nonchalance. For good measure I said, "Maybe now you'll believe me when I tell you something. I'm no liar, Frank. Leave me alone to sleep."

Sheepishly, he backed out. I locked the eyehook on my door and dropped on the bed like a bag of cement, hoping only for the sweet release of sleep. That escape now eluded me. My dying neighbor's racking cough and congested breathing tormented me. It went on and on, noisy and nauseating. He was coughing his life away. I wondered if it was some alcoholic illness, a liver disease, or emphysema, tuberculosis, or maybe even cancer. In my misery, it was hard to spare him too much sympathy. I found myself more in harmony with the other voices that echoed down the hall.

Some resident shrieked from his cubicle. "Shut up! Goddamn you!" Surprisingly, in this hellhole, he was answered by a kinder, more understanding soul.

"Poor devil can't *fucken* help it, man, leave him alone! He'll be dead soon enough."

There was compassion even here. I swore I'd never drink so much again; it wasn't worth the misery. I couldn't imagine anyone wanting to be a wino. No, I'd stick to beer.

26

CRUISING LAFAYETTE PARK

hin-chin-chin-aling! My wind-up alarm clock jangled away. Having puked the poison out of my plumbing, morning found me feeling much better. I jumped up refreshed, ready for a hearty breakfast and another day of running around Jefferson Parish.

After pocketing the change on the dresser and combing my hair, I looked with trepidation between the bed and the wall. My purple vomit was already drying out and beginning to flake off. It didn't smell bad, not with all the other odors abounding there and I thought it was kind of pretty, a nicer color than the faded industrial green paint it covered. I didn't feel like cleaning it up right away. Maybe I'd leave my puke painted wall as a parting gift to Frank when I left, as my thanks for his interrupting my precious sleep.

He'd given me back my money, but what burned me up was he hadn't given me the benefit of the doubt. He ought to trust me now and think twice before he banged on my door again. As an underage fugitive, I couldn't make a fuss and had to let it go.

Pancakes, bacon, and hot coffee went down great that morning. Johnny told the guys at work everything about the night before, and they ribbed me about it. The guy who'd first invited me to join the crew seemed amazed at my recovery.

"Don't ya even have a hangover, Jim?"

"Naw, I feel great!"

The old-timer of the group, muffled by his heavy parka, said, "Some guys just never get hangovers. They are God's warning, ya know, keeps some of us from becoming alcoholics."

Laughing and joking with the guys, I felt accepted, one of them. Bums were regular fellows once you got to know them. The older men, veterans of life's battles, had struck out too many times, but younger guys, like Johnny, were bouncing back from a personal crisis, insisting that they wouldn't stay on the skids for long. Who was I to judge? They were family now.

Johnny winked at me. "Jimbo, I got important things to do after work today. You'll be in on my plans soon enough, but you're on your own until morning."

After the freezing morning, we sweated through the afternoon, but New Orleans cooled off in the evening and I was getting used to the rhythm. With the rest of the day to myself, I crossed Girod and took a stroll around Lafayette Square. Although it was not the most cared for park, the grass needed to be replenished from the relentless foot traffic. But with its trees, I could forget I was smack in the middle of skid row. Relishing the breeze and communing with nature, I strolled along the sidewalk at the edge of the park. Still hoping for an adventure that involved a wild-spirited girl, I tried to figure out what to do with the rest of the day. Maybe I'd walk up to the French Quarter and see if I could slip past a bouncer into one of the clubs. Then a shiny white convertible with the top down, pulled over beside me, and the driver flashed me a breezy smile.

"Hi there, friend. Do you want a lift someplace?" He was a yellow-haired, handsome guy in his twenties, with an open-necked Hawaiian shirt, reminding me of Kookie, the hip character who was always combing his blond hair on 77 Sunset Strip, the television show I'd grown up with, but I was cautious at first.

"Naw, I'm just taking a walk. I live around here."

"What?" Kookie sounded surprised. "You live around *here*? You know this is a rough neighborhood, don't you? Anything could happen to you here."

"Everybody's got to live somewhere, don't they?" I felt protective of my neighborhood. It had become my refuge.

"Well, gee, how about going for a spin? Maybe we could talk or something?"

I sized him up. He didn't seem to be a cop. His smile was infectious, and this Kookie looked like he knew where we could pick up girls. New Orleans was proving to be a friendly town.

"Sure," I said as I hopped in. "I wasn't doing anything, anyway,"

"It sure is a nice day," he said. "Where are you from? You don't sound like a local boy."

"That's true," I said and left it at that.

"I worry about a good-looking boy like you living in this neighborhood. You look so young; you'd be *so* attractive to the older men here."

"It's okay. I got friends and can take care of myself."

"Since you're new in town, I'll show you some of the sights. Ever heard of Jean Lafitte the pirate?"

I nodded. "Sure, I know a lot about history. He and Andrew Jackson stopped the British invasion here in the War of 1812."

He pointed to a dilapidated gray plank building we were passing. "That's his tavern over there. One of several places he's said to have owned. I'll bet you haven't been across the Mississippi River yet?"

"Sure, I have."

"Not this far south you haven't, Yankee boy! It's a darn big river down here."

I'd just been over that bridge an hour ago, but Kookie wanted to impress me, so I let him. This time, I didn't have to peer out from under a truck's canopy. I took in the full panorama of the mighty river. The barges and tugboats were mere toys in this huge bathtub, and the setting sun painted shimmering colors on the otherwise brown river below. Kookie relished the role of a tour operator. Maybe that's what he did for a living.

"This is the Greater New Orleans Bridge, an engineering marvel. It cost something like sixty-five million dollars to build. It's over two miles long, the longest bridge in the whole United States." He glanced at me, and I tried to appear suitably impressed. "Right here in the middle. It arches to 170 feet above the river."

"Yeah, wow," I said, surprised at his knowledge of the details. "It really takes your breath away, man."

On the other side, we swung through the same neighborhoods I'd been working in all week, but I didn't mention that. As it got dark, my host led our conversation along a predictable path. He asked me about school, sports, and then girls, from inane topics he zeroed in on sex.

"Have you ever gotten a girl to *go down* on you?"

"How far down do you mean?"

He laughed. "Down between your legs, silly boy! Have you ever gotten a blowjob?"

Afraid to make a fool of myself, I tried to shrug off the question. Breathlessly, he pressed me for details. *Do you like to be on top or the bottom? What sort of positions have you tried? Would you like to have some great sex right now?*

"Sure, man, let's find some girls!"

"You look so young, so good looking. I'll bet the girls really go for you!" He said that as if it was an objective fact, but it embarrassed me. I only wished it were so, because so far, my looks hadn't opened any girls' hearts.

"Well, I've never had sex or even a real girlfriend."

"What, a handsome boy like you? You never had any experience with a woman?"

"No," I said, hoping my luck was about to change. "But I'd sure like to try. I've read about how wild New Orleans used to be in Storyville and the French Quarter, but where are the wild girls now? There must still be something like a red-light district left around here."

He ignored my question. "How about man-sex? Ever tried it?"

The question took me off guard. Did he mean what I thought he did? I hadn't pegged him for a homosexual. He pulled into a service station and turned to me, batting his eyelashes like a coquettish schoolgirl. We were far from any part of town I recognized, or I would have jumped out of the car and run.

"I have to use the powder room, Dearie," he said with a voice that had changed to a woman's flirtatious lilt, deferential, like a submissive wife to her adored lord and master. "Would you ask the man to fill me up, please?" The double meaning made me blush.

What made it more embarrassing was the attendant stood there and must have heard every word. As he stood up, I noticed for the first time that Kookie was unnaturally broad in the beam for a man. His hips were rounded and as fleshy as a woman in tailored trousers. He wriggled them provocatively as he swayed, rolling his hips in an exaggerated imitation of a woman's flirtatious walk. He craned his neck around to catch my reaction, smiled and winked at me. Grinning lasciviously, he sashayed slowly to the toilet.

The attendant, a regular sort of late teenage guy, stood with his mouth agape in shock. "Jesus, did you see *that*?"

I must have looked as dumbfounded as he did. Then he asked me the million-dollar question. "Excuse me for asking, but is that guy a queer or something?" Like he thought I should know. This was all new to me, but yes, this was exactly how a *queer* would act. What a fine mess I'd gotten myself into. Even though I'd never see this stranger again, I needed to make it clear that I wasn't a homo.

"He's just giving me a ride," I said. "I really don't know him."

"Oh no, I mean, I wasn't trying to say *you* were a queer or anything."

Kookie came back, all smiles and flirtatious giggles. He paid the boy, who then backed off like he'd seen more than enough. Batting his eyelashes at me, Kookie got in on the driver's side, but sat closer to the middle, crowding me on my side of the seat, making me uncomfortable as he drove off, chattering away.

"Have you ever tried sex with a man? I mean, I like all kinds of sex myself, but I really like man-sex best. Would you like to try some man-sex right now?"

"No, thank you." I tried to keep my voice firm, my rejection clear without offending him. "I only like girls. If you like all kinds of sex, maybe we could find some girls." I was still hopeful of realizing the true promise of New Orleans, to taste a bit of the lure that had brought me there, but he ignored my request and kept after me.

"You really should try man-sex. I promise you'll like it. A man can give a much better blowjob than a woman because, with the same body, he knows what a guy likes."

"Nothing personal, man. I'm just not a homo. I only like girls."

"Please! I really, really, like you. You can stick it in my mouth or up my ass, spank me, slap me if you like. I'll let you do anything to me!"

If only he was a she. But the magic wasn't there for me with him. I stayed adamant in my rejection, and he finally seemed to give up.

"Okay, honey, I promise I'll keep my hands to myself."

He slid back over onto the driver's side and I took a deep breath to calm my nerves, and he kept talking.

"I'll be a perfect gentleman and drive you back home. If you change your mind, though, I'll do whatever you want. We can still be friends. I do like to have friends, you know."

"Sure, we could be friends. Why not? We're just people, so long as you keep your hands to yourself."

I wasn't sure what being friends with him would entail. Kookie had started out in my imagination as a lady's man, not a man-lady. It was disappointing how this little joyride had turned out, but no harm was done. In fact, I saw this as an educational experience, seeing up close and personal someone whose desires did not match mine.

Maybe I had to overcome my aversion and try to understand more about the complex human condition. I was becoming interested in what made people tick. Homosexuals surrounded me in New Orleans. Could I even be sure that Johnny wasn't one? What if I was the only heterosexual left in the whole city? That thought was too depressing to consider. I hungered for sex as much as Kookie did, but not with a man.

We reached the familiar streets of my run-down, bad part of town, as Kookie called it and Skid row welcomed me with a homelike feeling. But instead of dropping me where he'd picked me up, Kookie insisted on taking me to my place. He still didn't believe that I lived around there and claimed to be worried about my safety. Maybe he just wanted to know where to look for me again, but I wasn't sure that would be a good idea.

"Stop right here." I said when we were still a block from my hotel, but he kept circling around the park and only pulled to the curb when we were exactly across the street from my hotel. Had he guessed where I lived?

There wasn't any other traffic and Frank and a few residents I knew were standing around by the entrance, watching us with blank, bored faces. I didn't want to get out under their scrutiny, but Kookie began making a last forlorn plea.

"You ought to at least try man-sex once, *please*. I can give you a great blowjob, you'll love it." He said that too loud, maybe audibly, to my attentive friends, and that got on my nerves.

"Sorry, man, I've gotta go!" I said as I jumped over the unopened door of the convertible and waited until he drove off before I crossed the street. Frank and the others stared at me without smiling. I wondered what they could be thinking.

"Man, what a ridiculous guy that was!" I said, for their benefit. Then my pent-up emotions exploded in an insane laugh that only made my audience stare the more. Maybe they thought I was high on something, but why should I care what a bunch of bums thought? I'd already paid my Buck-fifty for the day, so the ever grim and humorless Frank just watched me, steely eyed, as I passed him on my way inside. Fuck him, I thought, and another bellyful of laughter ripped out of me, causing me to double over. I gave up trying to hold it in and laughed all the way to my room. The whole event was hilarious. New Orleans was a fucking scream when you came right down to it.

27

BLACK AND WHITE AND THE BAREFOOT GIRL

I t was white paint brushed onto a red brick wall. Written in a shaky, misspelled scrawl, as if a child had done it, but at my eye level, which was too high for a very young child to reach.

Fuck niggers! get the hell out town now!

you nut belong here niether!

go back in aferca were you belongs!

This screed would be comical if it wasn't so nasty. Johnny shook his head and said, "Whoever scrawled that shit probably came from somewhere else. New Orleans is not prejudiced. We're the most mixed, tolerant place in the Deep South, but there are idiots and fools everywhere you go in this world."

I'd noticed very few blacks among the winos and derelicts where we lived on Skid Row. Working for Robeson Advertising, I didn't see a single black face until my second week, when the two of them came together and worked on our crew. One of them looked as young as I was. He got dropped off to work in the same neighborhood with Johnny and me. When I got to the pickup point, the black kid told me that Johnny, always up for earning a little more, had already been picked up to finish another area. The new kid was exhausted on his first day and he wouldn't say much. Maybe he too was a runaway. I asked him straight out, and his eyes looked away as he said, "No, I'm just new in town, is all."

But he seemed to be hiding something. Finally, he told me he was from a rural area outside of the city, staying in New Orleans with an aunt and working to earn his keep. That matched my cover story to a tee. The truck finally came back to pick us up, ending my only conversation with a guy my age who was almost certainly in the same situation as I was.

New Orleans hadn't been the vivacious sexual wonderland I'd hoped for. Surrounded by down on their luck men without a woman, I saw few opportunities to meet any kind of woman or girl. Only homosexuals and female impersonators made themselves available and strutted their stuff.

"Relax!" Johnny told me over and over. "We'll go see my little barefoot girl on Saturday night. That's when she works at the bar around the corner. She's a wild one, alright." He pretended to size me up and snickered. "She just might go for a handsome young buck like you."

Saturday came at last. We turned left on St. Charles and went into the second bar. The ever-present musty odor of this humid climate mixed with the pungent smell of stale beer and sweat. Country music played on the jukebox. *Son of a gun, we'll have big fun on the bayou...* Jambalaya, a Hank Williams song, celebrated the rollicking Cajun fun I hoped to find.

Pallid and voluptuously plump, the barmaid stood behind her bar with sublime confidence, in firm charge of her all-male patrons. Her unkempt stringy blond hair hung over her shoulders, damp with sweat in the un-air-conditioned establishment. She was busy working, of course, hardly at her best, but a wonderful sight for my eyes.

Johnny and I bellied up to the crowded bar. He leaned over and pointed down at her feet, and sure enough, she was barefoot.

We had to shout to be heard over the music. Johnny said, "She doesn't worry about no dirty floor or broken glass, Jimbo. She's a real toughie, that one, just the way I like my women."

He waved her over and said, "Hey Darlin, how're we doing tonight?"

She hoisted a full pitcher of foaming beer in each hand, which caused her full-size breasts to jut forward in her clinging, sweat-stained, almost transparent blouse. She was not a perfectly proportioned Playboy model, nor an innocent schoolgirl, but much more. She was an Earth Goddess, the gritty image of a real woman who understood men and their needs, but, unfortunately for Johnny and me, an exasperated grimace crossed her face.

"Look, Johnny. I don't have time for any of your shit right now." She marched to the other end of the long bar. Over her shoulder, she called back. "Can't you see that I'm busy tonight?"

She rounded the bar to carry her full load of foaming nectar to a table in the back, where she laughed and lingered with a couple of better dressed men. One of them took her elbow, and she sat down on his lap for a while with her arm on his shoulder.

Johnny and I took a newly vacated table in the front. "Don't worry about that little tantrum," he said, seemingly unruffled by her cold welcome. "She's a hot number. Just needs a little convincing." He winked and nudged me. "When I get my winnings, I'll flash some cash her way. That'll get her interested."

When the barefoot girl finally came back, she distractedly took our order for a pitcher and hurried off. She made herself scarce to us, taking a more professional interest in the needs of men at the other tables, laughing at whatever they said. She belatedly brought us our pitcher, but didn't stick around to lavish as much time on Johnny and me as she did the others, who must have tipped well, and we didn't order a second pitcher when that was gone.

His barefoot dream-girl's cold shoulder made Johnny quieter than usual. "Let's go, Jimbo." He led me to a few other places, but everywhere we went there were only men, with but a very few bent, haggard, and dried out crones to represent the fair sex.

"Don't you think we ought to look somewhere else, Johnny, like in the French Quarter?"

He gave me a sour smile. "Sure, Jimbo. There're plenty of women there. We just can't afford 'em right now. But I promise you, we'll get to them in good time."

In good time. I was damn tired of hearing that, but as a runaway, I was in no position to charge out there all by myself, only to get arrested or bilked out of all I possessed. Johnny was looking out for me, and I had to let him call the shots.

"Truth is, Jimbo, we got to flash a bigger bankroll than either of us got. At present, that is. No way will we make enough at our paper-pushing job, but there're other ways to make money."

He launched into a long-winded explanation of his job as a dealer, how he'd learned a few tricks that could increase his take. But not being a card player, it all went over my head. I didn't have a lot of choice *but* to trust him. So far, he'd played straight with me and given me no cause for alarm. He had plans that included me to make us both more cash than our dead-end jobs.

Johnny put his arm around me. "Just you wait and see, my man. Before long, things will look up. We'll be rolling in the green and the women will be lining up to be with us."

28

SUNDAY, 28 MAY: CHURCHMEN

Johnny banged on my door. "Come on Jimbo! Let's get a move on. We have to hurry to get a place in line."

I woke up, and my alarm clock told me it wasn't even six o'clock.

"What's all the fuss, Johnnie? It's Sunday morning. We don't have work today."

"Work?" His voice rose in mock surprise. "Who said anything about work? There's a free feed every Sunday at the Catholic shelter. On our income, it'd be a shame to miss it."

Johnny was always looking for an angle. I didn't need convincing, but he went into his justifications. "I don't see myself as a freeloader, Jimbo. I help 'em out down there. It's as much a social outing as a meal for us."

The Ozanam Inn, at 829 Camp Street, was run by the St. Vincent de Paul organization, located just a block from the Camp Inn, where we usually ate dinner. We joined a long line of ragged men, no women in sight, to pass slowly into a great dining hall. The salt and pepper bearded men, wearing tattered and disheveled clothing, sat themselves around long tables. We were waited on by trusties, some of their own.

These better dressed, rehabilitating down-and-outers, worked under the supervision of two brown-robed monks. The food was filling, scrambled eggs, stacks of toast, and oatmeal, with pitchers of water, juice and coffee spaced at regular intervals along the tables.

Johnny spoke quieter, much more subdued than usual, as he chatted with the men beside him and gave cheerful greetings to the monks, who he knew by name, and he didn't seem to mind the brief religious service that went with the meal. His last name, Marino, sounded Spanish or Italian, so I assumed he was raised a Catholic, but if so, he was a lapsed Catholic because he never went to confession or attend mass. He was honest about his personal failures with me and waxed philosophic about human nature and gave me his assessment of what had brought each of the men around us to this point in their lives.

"It's usually booze that drives these guys to the skids, Jimbo, but miserable jobs, bitchy wives, and family troubles push them to drink in the first place."

He grew wistful and stirred his coffee. "That's true with me too, Jimbo. It sure don't pay to cast stones or play holier than thou with other people. I'm on the mend now. By this time next year, things will be different. For you too, 'cause you're my partner and we gotta look out for each other."

The monks padded around on sandals behind the scenes, unobtrusively directing the trusties with their meal and clean-up duties. I was curious about the monks, and Johnny said I ought to chat with them.

"These brothers are good fellows. They're not just dogmatic Catholics, Jimbo. They've got some interesting ideas and are well read on a wide range of topics. We'll stay after we eat to help them clean up."

As most of the others filed out, Johnny and I went into the kitchen with Brother Andrew. He handed us cleaning supplies and sent us to work in different areas. While I began scrubbing down the large walk-in cooler, affable Brother Andrew came in and chatted while helping me. He was in his mid-twenties. The crown of his head was shaved, leaving a rim of dark black hair around the sides. I asked him about this.

"You mean my tonsure? That's part of my uniform, like my robes." He chuckled. "I've taken vows of poverty, chastity, and obedience, to live in service to God and serve his creatures." He fixed me with a serious look. "Are you a Christian?"

I had strong views on the matter. "I believe in reincarnation, more of a Hindu or a Buddhist than a Christian." I expected him to attack my ideas, like Christians usually did with any alternate vision of spirituality, but he nodded and said he was open-minded about that concept, so I went on.

"But I've got nothing against Jesus. In fact, I think he must have gotten his more universal ideas from those older religions. Judaism started out as a mean, tribal religion under a bloodthirsty satanic god, bent on genocide to take their promised land from the Canaanites."

He laughed. "Well, that's quite a concept. I see you have read your Bible thoroughly. Have you ever heard of Thomas Merton?"

"Yes, I heard he was some kind of beatnik Trappist monk, always in trouble with the church."

He laughed. "I bet you would get a lot out of reading his books. His Seven Storey Mountain is inspiring. Maybe I can find a copy of it for you to read next time you come. We Catholics are a more diverse, open-minded bunch than you might think."

Brother Andrew was the first monk I'd spoken with. He seemed well informed, not a fanatic, like I was used to back home. He guessed I was a runaway but told me that was between me and my god, whoever that was. As we finished up, he shook my hand.

"Thanks for the interesting conversation. If you ever need anything, even if it's just someone to talk to, don't hesitate to come here. We're not the police, you know, we're servants of God."

We came back for another meal and chat the following Sunday in June. These monks seemed to be decent fellows, and little by little, I relaxed my guard around them.

29

WEDNESDAY, JUNE 7, 1967: THE GRAND SLAM

"Tonight's the night, Jimbo. I'll show you the sweet deal I'm working on. There's no sense going back to our hotel. We'll be out the whole night and won't bother going to work in the morning," Johnny said after we got our pay.

I'd known Johnny for two weeks, but I was still having trouble following his breathless monologs. Later, I'd try to rewind the tape in my head to make better sense of the torrent of words he'd spewed at me. He claimed to be a dealer, but it wasn't drugs. He'd said something about shuffling cards, so I conjured up images from old movies. I imagined him as a guy with a hatless visor on his forehead and black sleeves on his forearms, beneath the glare of a bare light bulb. He'd be dealing out cards to a room full of poker-faced men chomping cigars, but I had no idea how I was going to fit into that scenario. He'd let me sit in on it first to get an idea.

Straight from work, we marched over to our favorite haunt, the Camp Inn. Johnny was his exuberant self as we ate big slices of pizza and sipped glasses of Dixie. He shot me a knowing wink.

"It's going to be a packed house tonight, Jimbo. We'll make a killing and tomorrow we'll wash up and go out on the town. I promised I'd get you laid, didn't I? Well, flush with cash in our pockets, you'll get your trip around the world and sample some of those bearded clams I've been telling you about!"

We laughed and clinked our bottles of Dixie together. Then he got serious.

"There's only one small catch, Jimbo. We need to sweeten the pot. With a little extra, about thirty bucks each, we'll increase our stake in the jackpot. We're in this deal together, ya know."

He grabbed my forearm and gave me a sincere look. "This is a loan with interest, mind you. You'll be paid back many times over before the night is over."

We'd come this far together, and I had to trust him, so I reached into my pocket, dug out my cash, and counted it up. "I've got two Tens, and two Fives in cash."

Johnny clapped his hands. "That's thirty bucks on the nose, a lucky omen, Jimbo." He snatched up the bills. "You've done the right thing."

I nodded, hoping he was right. After getting robbed on my first night in the city and not claiming the money Tom owed me, this was all I'd managed to save, thirty dollars and some loose change that jangled in my other pocket. But a guy had to start somewhere. Johnny talked about us sharing a big apartment where we could bring girls, just like what Tom and I talked about. The difference was that Tom was an old drunk, and didn't seem as likely as Johnny to reel in a girl, or pay his way.

Although I hated to part with my dough, I knew any success in life demanded taking risks. Risk had gotten me to New Orleans. All my current job gave me was a hand to mouth existence. Although I tried to save, dollar by dollar, it got spent on life's necessities: food, rent, and beer ate it up. I didn't want to live hand to mouth forever, but with Johnny as my partner, I'd be sure to turn my luck around and prosper in the Big Easy.

Johnny looked at his watch. "It's time to go, Jimbo." We walked several blocks to a flophouse with no name. An ancient, weathered sign painted high on the red brick wall read: "30 cents a day."

"Gee, Johnny, this place is cheaper than the Girod Hotel."

Johnny chuckled. "Forget it, Jimbo! That sign goes back to the Depression era. It's still a bughouse, costs more like sixty cents or a dollar now, but all they offer is a bare cot in a big, packed dormitory, and you really gotta watch your stuff surrounded by winos."

We entered the building and climbed up a steep flight of stairs to the grungy lobby. About twenty men stood around the clerk's desk. That sweaty, burly, and bearded man wore a sleeveless tee shirt exposing his massive biceps. He stood behind his tall podium fiercely, eyeing everyone as they came past him.

Johnny gave him a familiar wave and a smile. "There's two of us today, Carl." Without stopping, we breezed on towards a heavy steel door on the far side of the room. The door was half open; a dark stairwell led up to where I supposed the night's action was to be.

"Hold it right there, Johnny." Carl's face flushed crimson. "Where do you think you're going with that kid?"

Johnny wheeled around, his eyes wide in surprise, and he launched into a determined counterattack. "Look, Carl, I been coming here regularly for a long time now. You know me; I can vouch for this guy. There'll be no trouble here tonight. I swear."

"Well, you can go up, Johnny, but you're not bringing that god-dammed kid in there!" Wham! He slammed his ham fist on the desk.

Johnny turned to me. "Don't worry, I'll handle this." He tried everything. Demanding, threatening, and finally pleading, to no avail. Only bluffing was left.

"Come on, Jimbo!" he called over his shoulder as he strode purposefully to the forbidden doorway.

Our bellicose clerk roared. "Stop those guys!"

One of the men, more terrified of the burly clerk than of us, slammed and bolted the door before us and then slipped out of our way. None of these men looked eager for a fight, but if it came to that, it was obvious whose side they would be on. What the hell was I getting myself into? I couldn't afford a scene that could involve the cops and blow my cover.

Carl wouldn't back down and looked ready for a rumble.

"Goddamn it, Johnny, I can't let a young kid up there, with a roomful of fucking old men. Not on my watch. I won't allow it!"

Now I was angry. Did this bastard take me for a homosexual? I was suddenly aware of everyone's eyes on me. I felt myself reddening with embarrassment.

Carl shrieked, banging his countertop. "Get that damn kid out of here now or I'll throw you both out!" The bear of a man was big enough to tear us limb from limb.

"Sorry Jimbo." For once, Johnny sounded shaken. "Don't worry; I'll see you in the morning. Like I said, your money will get paid back with dividends. We'll be flush and go out on the town." His voice softened, filled with obvious concern. "You sure you got enough dough on you for tonight, partner?"

Without bothering to check my pockets, I reassured him. "Oh yeah, I've got a bunch of change." I jiggled the coins in my pocket. "It should be plenty." All I needed was to get the hell away from Carl and all this unwanted commotion.

"See you in the morning," Johnny said as he vanished into the reopened stairway, and the crowd of men streamed after him. The last man in shut and bolted the heavy door from within. Tonight, our big moneymaking night was in Johnny's hands.

Under the withering gaze of Carl, who stood like the guard dog at the gates of Hades, I retreated into the hot Louisiana sunshine. It burned me up. I was just a kid, nothing in the eyes of the world. It wasn't fair.

On the threshold of my hotel, Frank, the other manager from hell, blocked my way. I fished in my pocket and dumped my coins on the counter. Three quarters, five dimes, three nickels and two pennies tallied up to a buck forty two. I was eight cents short, less than a dime.

"Sorry Frank, I'm short a few cents, but I'll make it up tomorrow."

Frank's serious eyes drilled into me. "Look Jim, I don't give a shit about tomorrow. It's a buck and a half each and every night. Get it? Pay up or ya don't get in!"

"Well Frank, remember the time you roused me out of bed for the rent I already paid? I've never once been short. Just let me in to get some rest and I promise I'll make it up to you with interest in the morning. Johnny will be back then and he owes me money, too."

He shook his head. I had to come up with something else, but I still couldn't take the situation seriously.

"What can I give you for collateral?" I emptied my pockets. "Look, here's a brown buck knife, and a yellow handled fish cleaning knife." They were gifts from my granddad, the only treasures of my meager existence, worth far more than a dime, but he still wouldn't budge.

"Okay, let me get my wind-up alarm clock from the room. That's worth something."

He shook his head. "I don't need your cheap trash, Jim."

Half joking, I lifted my leg onto the counter and began untying my shoelaces. "Okay Frank, how about my shoes, then? They're brand new." I had put some miles on those crepe shoes, but I needed to show Frank how ridiculous this situation was.

"Get your foot off my counter. I don't want your goddamn shoes, kid. Go out and get me the full buck-fifty and you can get in."

Out of options, I trekked back to the bughouse where I'd left Johnny. Before Carl could even open his mouth, I blurted out: "Look, I only want to have a quick word with Johnny, and I'll be gone."

Carl blew up. "You? Back again! Goddamn it, kid. I know what you're up to, you little cocksucker. I'll never let a punk kid like you in on my watch."

That slimy bastard's suggestion that I was queer pissed me off. Fuck him. I didn't need this. I had dignity, goddamn it. With my head held high, I marched out of there and hiked the length of Girod Street, begging for pennies whether as a loan or gift. I knew most of these guys by sight and had worked with some. They looked at me like I was crazy, panhandling in this neighborhood, but I was afraid that if I did this on the posh side of town, I'd wind up arrested for sure. If I tried sleeping away in an alley, that was certain to happen. I was at my wit's end and getting frantic. A grizzled old guy had a better idea.

"Why don't you just go over to the mission? They'll put you up until morning."

That looked like my only option. Brother Andrew seemed like an approachable, reasonable guy. So, like the Hunchback of Notre Dame in that old movie I watched as a kid, I'd take refuge in Mother Church.

30

BETWEEN JESUS AND MARY AND A
HOT PLACE IN HELL

The Mission on Camp Street was ready to close its doors for the night when I arrived. The friendly face of Brother Andrew greeted me. I asked him straight out for a ten-cent loan.

"I'm sorry, Jim. We don't have any money at all. You see, we follow a strict vow of poverty here and don't keep any money on hand in the mission."

"Come on, somebody has to have a measly dime tucked into the pocket of a robe. I'll pay it back tomorrow."

"We feed and shelter derelict men, who are prone to sin and might rob us, therefore we keep no money here and spare them from temptation. Our lay members handle all purchases and financial matters and they have gone home for the night. Why don't you stay the night here? We've finished accepting overnighters, but I'll squeeze you in."

"Great, all I need is to get through the night."

"Brother Michael will handle you from here. My shift is over." He passed me into the hands of a monk I didn't know.

Brother Michael took his job seriously, ordering me to hand over my valuables. That was the easy part; I didn't have anything but my watch and pocketknives. Then I was given a form to fill out. It asked for my home address and background. Keeping my alias of Jim Hassle, I let my imagination run, making up an address in Cleveland. Surely, they wouldn't bother to verify any of this. How many of these derelict men reported all these details correctly? They'd only check to see that all the blanks were filled in. I doubted if many of these derelict men could even remember enough of their former lives to report all these details correctly.

Brother Michael told me to wait on a folding chair in a long hallway. The other bums were finished bedding down by that time, while waited alone, trying not to fidget or appear nervous. A harried monk came running by and I reached out to him. "Why am I still waiting?"

"The monsignor wants to have a personal interview with you."

"Why do I get a personal interview and not those other guys?"

"You are not in our system. It's just a formality." He hurried off.

There I sat, another stray sheep in their pasture, awaiting my turn to be shorn and turned in with the flock. Maybe I was being paranoid, but the situation seemed fishy, and I wondered if I should make a break for it. The doors had been securely bolted. Attempting to run out could cause a stir and backfire on me. Panic was my enemy.

At last, a door opened, and a monk approached. "The monsignor will see you now." He ushered me into a tidy office.

The Monsignor was an older, lanky, white-haired man, dressed in civilian clothes, rather than the drab brown robes of his underlings. Without a word of greeting, he riveted me with hard eyes for a long minute as his smile slowly turned into a sneer. His silent treatment was unsettling. He reminded me of my principal back in school who'd pegged me for a troublemaker and tried to unnerve me this way. This church official, too, seemed to be used to exerting authority over errant mortals. He glanced down at the form in his hand, then back at me.

Breathing deep and exhaling slowly, I did my best to keep cool and restrain my natural exuberance, hiding my emotions under the façade of indifference, as if I was older, a man of eighteen, but that was a hard job after my nerve-wracking day.

"So, you're Jim Hassle from Toledo, are you?" He slouched back in his comfortable swivel chair, behind the barricade of his desk. As he did so, I could see that the form he held was the one I'd filled out.

I answered glib and upbeat. "That's me all right."

"That's strange." He peered at me over the form in his hand. "You just said 'yes' to Toledo, but it says here that you lived in Cleveland, Ohio?"

The bastard was trying to spook me. I hadn't expected such a grilling and berated myself for answering too fast.

"Well, uh, sure, but we moved a lot. I can't remember all the addresses."

"Is that so? So, you lived at, ah, what's that address again?"

I'd forgotten what I'd put on the form and was squirming under the microscope of his piercing gray-blue eyes. He waited with smug satisfaction for an answer that he knew I didn't have.

"Not sure where you lived?" He raised his voice ironically. "Give me what you *do* remember then, because you see, my friend, I've been to Cleveland *and* Toledo, and I know them well."

His malevolent smile reminded me of a cat toying with a canary under its paw. He asked me about side streets, schools I attended, and the local landmarks of Cleveland.

"I just made that up," I admitted, angry at myself for screwing up. Having read books on clandestine operations, I should have concocted a thorough cover identity ready before I ran away, but kept putting it off. The show must go on, however, even if I'd blown my lines.

His smile broadened even more. "So, you are an admitted liar." He let the form drop from his hand and it glided onto his desk. The bastard thought he was slick, playing Gestapo with me. It was hard not to hate him and all he stood for. He was the grand inquisitor with a heretic in his dungeon. I wanted to tell him off, but restrained myself. Better not get into it with this pompous ass right now.

"Look, sir," I said. "I've committed no crime. I only came here because I knew Brother Andrew. All I needed was a loan of a few pennies. Instead, he offered me shelter for the night. Who do you think I am? A Commie spy?"

He didn't laugh or even crack a smile, so I sailed on. "Okay, this isn't worth the hassle. I'll just leave." I started to get up.

He sneered. "Leave? That won't be necessary or even possible, now. None of our guests is allowed in or out after the doors are secured. You can stay here, of course. Our work is to assist those in need, both temporally and spiritually." He pushed a buzzer and waved his hand to the door. "Brother Theodore will take you upstairs."

Maybe the Monsignor just wanted to put me through the ringer, break me down, and turn me into a blithering, repentant sinner, a fresh convert in the stable of the Lord Almighty. I followed the sandal-clad monk up a dark staircase. When we reached the top, he shushed me.

"We have to whisper; the men are sleeping."

He ushered me into a long, silent room full of narrow cots lined up in rows, where he gave me over to another monk standing like a silent sentinel. It seemed that I had gone back in time to another century. Each end of the long, high-ceilinged room was lit by votive candles, producing an eerie effect of flickering shadows on the walls. At one end of the room was a giant statue of a risen Christ, holding open his torn chest to expose his sacred heart, which glistened gory red in the flickering light. On the other side of the room stood a comparably sized statue of Mother Mary, gazing with sorrow upon her adoring children with a mother's love, wordlessly promising relief. If only we would surrender to her son and his wrathful, pitiless father. But I'd already had a bellyful of Christianity, Catholic or otherwise.

Old men lay motionless on all but the one empty cot in the middle that the monk directed me to. I almost sat down before he stopped me.

"You need to shower first." His harsh whisper indicated that I should have known that.

"Okay," I said. "A shower would be nice."

He led me to a gleaming white-tiled bathroom off to the side. The only trouble was I had nothing clean to put on afterwards. Hoping they offered some kind of robe, I put the towel around my waist and stepped out of the shower room.

The scandalized monk waved me back inside. "This is not a high school locker room!"

After I put my grungy duds back on, I felt only half clean.

The brother led me back to my bunk, where I kicked off my crepe shoes and lay down, fully clothed. He warned me. "Please try not to excite the passions of these men." The monk then padded away on his rounds. He circled the room like a sentry before he took up a post at one end of the room. There he stood, like an alabaster statue, for some minutes, before resuming his circumambulations. It reminded me of Zen walking meditation, which I'd recently read about.

My mind replayed the events of the day, and I couldn't sleep. Things had gone wrong so fast. My luck was bound to change once I got through this awful night and saw Johnny. Like him, I considered myself a survivor, not a victim. I'd left Ron the loser behind in Illinois, to remake myself as Jim, the bold adventurer, and had to accept with courage whatever came my way.

After an hour of contemplating the cosmos and my place in it, I'd almost drifted into sleep when I heard another pair of sandals climbing the stairs. I strained to listen as a short, whispered conference ensued with our vigilant guardian monk. Then both monks made their way to my cot. A hand gently, yet insistently, shook my shoulder.

"Hassle, get up, the Monsignor wants to see you."

"What, again?" Hadn't that smug brother superior grilled me enough? "What does he want?"

"You will find out."

A hell of an answer. They obeyed orders from their superiors without question.

"Couldn't this wait until morning?"

"No, you must come promptly."

I slipped on my shoes and followed him down, hoping to get this thing over with so I could snatch a few winks. I had a lot to look forward to in the morning. I wanted to be well rested for the promised day of celebration with Johnny. He'd promised to introduce me to the wild women of my dreams.

My escort knocked on the office door. "I have Mr. Hassle here to see you."

"Send him in."

The door opened on my antagonist, sitting behind his desk with a serene, self-satisfied smile. Without rising, he pointed to an empty chair opposite. Entering, I saw it was flanked by two casually dressed men in their mid-twenties. I didn't need anyone to tell me that they were cops. The bastard had turned me in.

31

BETRAYAL

With as much bravado as I could muster, I took the hot seat between the cops. The Monsignor wasted no time on pleasantries. "Mr. Hassle, I know you are lying. I doubt Hassle is your real name, and I know you are underage. Therefore, I have asked these gentlemen from the Juvenile division here to meet you." Beaming radiantly, he sat back and put his fingers together in a pyramid, pleased with his betrayal of my trust. The cops took up where he left off.

"All we want is for you to tell us the truth," said the blond one with a smile, as if he was on my side. "Your parents must be worried sick. After we contact them, we might let you go."

I'd read about police interrogation techniques. They'd operate in pairs. One would act as the good cop, to gain the prisoner's trust, and the other would play the bully. Sure enough, the dark-haired cop wore a mean frown, staring at me with angry eyes.

"If you don't cooperate and tell us who you really are, kid, you'll be going down to the station with us until we get some answers, and we will get them." He loomed over me and cleared his throat. "One way or the other, and it won't be pretty."

"Fess up and come clean, kid," said the good cop. "You might get out of this mess, and go home where you belong."

"I've committed no crime," I said, keeping my voice as calm as I could, but the bad cop had a ready answer. "Running away *is* a crime, kid. Your parents are legally responsible for you. You'd better tell us your real name, kid, because our conversation won't be as pleasant down at the station." His eyes narrowed with implied violence, and I knew Chicago cops beat recalcitrant prisoners with a rubber hose because it hurt like hell and didn't leave marks. My sixth-grade teacher, Mr. Trotter, threatened us with his own rubber hose, and I remembered how much it hurt when he turned it on me.

My tactics needed to change. If I played along with them, maybe they would let me go, or I might catch them off guard.

"Okay, you got me." I coughed up my real name, age, and home address. The bad cop excused himself and left the room. His blond partner chatted away, trying to keep me talking.

"You did the right thing, kid, saving us a long night of interrogation."

His partner returned, smiling. "Everything checked out. We just wanted your poor parents to know you are alright."

"Can I go back upstairs now and get some sleep?"

They looked at each other. Then the good cop faced me. "We'll take you to a better place. The mean streets of New Orleans are no place for you. You'll only get yourself into more trouble. Believe me, we're on your side, kid."

Although I'd done what they asked, I was still their prisoner, and they made no attempt to disguise it. The Monsignor handed them my belongings that included my brown buck knife and yellow handled fish cleaning knife, cherished gifts from my grandfather.

The blond asked. "Just what did you intend to do with these?"

"Self-defense," I said, hoping to get a laugh. When he frowned, I said. "What the heck do you think? They're just ordinary pocketknives, useful tools. I might do some fishing."

"You could hurt someone," he said. "We'll keep these."

"What? No, I've had them for years. My granddad gave them to me when I was ten-years-old, for God's sakes."

"These weapons are contraband." The bad cop took them without giving me a receipt.

"What are you going to do with them?"

"We'll throw them away."

That hurt. It would be an awful waste of Granddad's gift. I hoped they at least gave them to someone who could appreciate them.

The cops and the monsignor shook hands, congratulating themselves on a job well done. Sandwiched between the cops, they led me out. My last glimpse of the grand inquisitor, his smug face contorted in a self-righteous smile, incensed me. He'd earned my contempt for him and the religion he stood for.

One cop always held my belt at my back as we walked. They locked me in the back seat, but I hadn't been handcuffed. For the moment I played possum, speaking freely, joshing with them as I awaited a chance to make a break for it.

"Just where is that flop house where you live, kid?" said the bad cop with less tension in his voice.

"The Girod Street Hotel, just off St. Charles."

"Wait in the car while we get your stuff," said the blond cop as we pulled up in front. Frank came up and blinked in surprise when he saw me sitting in the back seat. He led them inside, but they returned in only a couple of minutes.

The bad cop looked exasperated. "You have a goddamn lock on your door. What's the combination?"

"I'll have to do it myself."

They let me out of the car and held my belt as they walked me in. Frank and a few bums watched, wondering what I'd done.

"What a dump!" the bad cop said. "This is no place for a kid like you. Jesus Christ, kid, did you grow up like this?"

"It isn't so bad. All I need is a place to flop and a roof over my head."

I unlocked the door and gathered up all I owned into one big bundle of clothes, including my alarm clock, but my captors, feeling uncomfortable in the surroundings that had been my refuge, rushed me.

"Hurry up and let's get the hell out of here! This place gives me the creeps."

Returning to the car, I chided the bad cop, who was tightly clutching my belt. "Are you afraid of a skinny kid like me? Am I some kind of dangerous felon?"

"Okay, kid, I'll let go if you promise not to run."

"Where the hell can I run to?"

As we descended the steps to the foyer, he let go of my belt and held the door open for me. *Not yet*, my brain insisted. Stay calm and steady. I counted in my mind: "One, two, three, now!" I dropped my burden and bolted to the left.

"Goddamn it, kid! Stop! Hold it right there!" The bad cop took off after me on foot. The other jumped behind the wheel of their car. Trying not to trip on the severely buckled pavement, I ran toward St. Charles. The cop running behind me stumbled and cursed. Several old bums stood ahead of me.

"Stop him! Get him!" the cop yelled, but the bums stepped aside to let me by. I whispered my breathless *thanks* as I ran by, and reached St. Charles, just as the light turned red. The cop car caught up beside me and the good cop jumped out after me.

For a split second, I considered running left up St. Charles, the wrong way on a one-way street, to get the car off my trail. Maybe I could duck into the barefoot girl's tavern and run out the back to lose them in the alley, but I didn't know if it was a dead end. With no time to weigh my options, I raced across the intersection, dodging the traffic that convinced the cop to race back to his car. Blasting the horn, he forced his way through traffic that screeched to a halt or ran up onto the curb to avoid him.

Halfway up the block, I reached the loading dock of the post office building. A couple of employees in summer uniforms were unloading a truck. One of them yelled. "What's all the commotion about, son?"

Maybe I should run into the loading dock, but the other doors were probably locked up, and I'd be trapped in there. The cop car screeched in front of me, cutting me off on the sidewalk. He threw it in park and leaped out at me. I dodged backwards, evading his grasp by inches. The running cop was closing in. Both were yelling and swearing.

"You goddamn son of a bitch, you're in for it now! Wait 'till we get you!"

I peeled away, across Girod into a rutted dirt parking lot with a few trees beside Lafayette Park. The car raced after me, bouncing over the curbs as I sprinted through the lot, berating myself for not running up St. Charles, as the car roared up from behind, cutting me off against a tree. Again, I evaded the driver's grasp and ran off at an angle as the runner closed in, herding me between them. When the car cut me off for a third time, I almost slammed into it just as the running cop came up from behind, boxing me in, with nowhere to run.

Wheezing, the running cop threw me onto the hood of the car and pulled my hands behind my back, shouting. "You goddamn punk!" The driver jumped out to help him, then slugged me in the small of my back.

I'd spoiled their day. In the dark, empty lot, they took their rage out on me. The angry bad cop was the worst, punching my side and back, and then he kicked my ass while his partner pinioned me on the hood. They threw me on the ground, twisting my arms high behind my back as they slapped handcuffs on me. The metal cuff on my left wrist felt loose, but the right cuff dug deep into my wrist bone.

"So, you wanna play rough, huh, kid? I'll give you rough!" The bad cop began kicking me again. "You like that, you goddamn punk?" After catching his breath, he tossed me, like a trussed-up animal, into the back seat, where I landed face first on the floor.

"Get up into that seat, goddamn you!"

With my arms behind my back, it was all I could do to wriggle up onto the seat while he continued kicking me.

"Hey, take it easy there, partner. That's all now. We don't want to bring him in too badly damaged," the good cop said.

That, I guessed, was why they only kicked and hit me on my back, not my face. Angry tears of humiliation and rage streamed down my face. They drove back to the street. The good cop turned to me with a worried, almost solicitous look.

"Are you okay, kid?"

My right wrist was in intense pain, but I wouldn't beg for mercy from these bastards. The good cop continued in a mild tone. "You asked for it, you know. You broke your promise and, well, it made us mad."

With every pothole and turn, the cuff dug into my right wrist. I tried to weave with the bouncing car but felt shooting pains up and down my arm. Eventually, it was replaced by a numbness, which worried me more. I twisted to hold my shoulders at an uneven angle that took some of the pressure off my wrist. My brain screamed, "Fuck them!" I'd lose my arm before I groveled before these cops.

They drove past my hotel. My belongings still lay where I'd dropped them. The manager and several of his tenants were standing around, amazement written on their faces.

The good cop said, "Should we pull over and pick up the kid's stuff?"

"To hell with that!" his partner said. "He threw his shit away. That's his fucking problem. This is going to be a long enough night for us. We still gotta fill out reports and take him to that fancy new lock-up across town."

I happened to be wearing Tom's gray baggy pants and the blue canvas crepe shoes I'd bought on my first day in town. They were all I had now as reminders of my independent life in New Orleans, which seemed to be over. On the drive to the police station, the bad cop mocked me.

"You're no tough guy, are you, kid? You're just a punk, is all. These nigger kids around here are tougher for us to deal with."

The good cop took my side. "He isn't such a bad kid. There's hope for him yet."

"Shit," his partner said, "These winos probably got him all messed up on drugs. He might be a heroin addict or something."

Still angry, I said nothing. They switched tactics, both becoming friendlier, trying to engage me in their banter, but I kept silent, clinging to a scrap of dignity.

We parked in front of the precinct station house in the black part of town. The only whites were officers of the law. Several black mothers were making a commotion on the steps, arguing with a white officer about whether their pre-teen boys deserved to be arrested. Still handcuffed, I was yanked to my feet and out of the car in front of this audience. Each movement brought fresh pain to my wrist. Limping, I struggled to twist my shoulders to take the weight off my right arm. As they led me through the melee, the mothers fell silent. After we passed through their ranks, their voices started up again.

A matron with her hair tied up in a kerchief put her hands over her mouth. "Oh, Lordy, you see dat boy. What you think he done? Kill somebody?"

Inside, we passed another black mother. She gasped when she saw me and turned to her surly son, a boy of about ten.

"You see dat?" She smacked him across the face. "You listen, brat! See what happen to you if you don mend your ways, like I been tellin you! You want ta tend up like him?"

I was an object lesson for the black youth of New Orleans. I laughed through gritted teeth as I imagined a screaming headline: "Vicious criminal arrested! Runaway Teen booked before the wide eyes of juvenile offenders and terrified mothers!"

The cops plopped me onto a wooden chair beside a desk in the middle of the busy station. Police and young offenders were coming and going. Telephones rang, and typewriters clicked all around us. My officers took turns sitting beside me at the desk and typing out their report. The other ran errands and brought his partner coffee. From time to time, they asked me questions. Still angry, I kept silent.

The injustice of my arrest irked me. I was a teenage runaway. So, what? Didn't the Constitution of this supposedly free country protect me? What about the Geneva Convention? It even protected enemy soldiers from abuse. The self-righteous establishment of priests and cops treated me like I was an enemy alien outside the rule of law. With their report typed up and turned in; my keepers heaved me to my feet and dragged me back to the car.

"We have a long drive ahead of us," the bad cop said in a whinny voice. "It looks like we'll be getting home late again."

It was too dark for me to make out landmarks as we drove out of the city. Waves of throbbing pain kept shooting through my right wrist. It became excruciating, then numb again. The mental anguish was worse. The cops began ribbing each other about how they almost let me get away.

"I can't believe how out of shape you are," the good cop said to his partner. "You better quit smoking, man."

"Easy for you to say. It was all you could do to keep up with him in the car!" He looked back at me. "Hey kid, you on drugs or something? A young guy like you should have gotten away easy from a bunch of old men like us."

They didn't look older than twenty-five, and their baiting didn't work. I refused to give them the pleasure of taking me down a peg. However, I agreed with them on one point. I should have gotten away. If I'd turned left on St. Charles, I might have lost them, but that was the luxury of hindsight. Even if I'd gotten away, I had nowhere to go, and it would only have been a matter of time before they flushed me out. No use beating myself up over it. The deck was stacked against me.

I was lucky to have lived on my own for as long as I did, and I still might get out of this somehow. Maybe Johnny would bail me out. Then I realized that would only get him in trouble for contributing to the delinquency of a minor.

We arrived at an antiseptic modern building that looked more like a hospital than a prison. Buzzed inside, the cops led me to an anteroom, where they felt safe enough to remove my cuffs. With difficulty, I brought my stiff arms in front. The pain returned with my circulation. Sharp needle pricks shot up and down my unresponsive right arm. It became excruciating.

"Oh god!" the officer who'd unbound me said. "Look at the kid's wrist, will you!"

There was a deep, quarter inch wide notch right over the wrist bone below my thumb where the cuff had dug in. The inch of skin around that was dark green; I wondered if it was gangrene. Another two inches out from that was greenish yellow, and the rest of my arm was beet red. The cops looked worried.

"Are you okay, kid?"

"Yeah, I'm just fine." I made my voice as sarcastic as Mom's when she talked to Dad.

"Rub it, kid," the good cop said with fright in his voice. "It'll be all right," He glanced at his partner. "Come on, let's get out of here. It's a long drive back."

They handed me off to a casually dressed, muscular black man with a cynical scowl, who led me through a labyrinth of halls and locked doors. I had to follow or be dragged. Each time he came to a door, he spoke into an intercom, saying something like "Counselor number five coming through."

After we were buzzed through, he said, "This place is state-of-the art, kid. We carry no keys for you to steal. If a councilor is overpowered and forced to speak, the stress in his voice will give it away. You can't escape this place." He chuckled like it was a joke on me. "Don't even think about it."

I felt trapped in an unfeeling machine with no way out. The regimented modern world was the enemy of mankind.

My counselor took me to a large, gleaming shower room. I said, "I already showered at the mission."

"It's the rules, kid. Ya'all gotta take one again."

For all my showering, I still had to dress in the same sweaty clothes I'd arrived in. He then led me to a small room, padded with soft blue plastic. The heavy door thudded shut behind me, muffling outside sounds. A dull light shone in through a thick Plexiglas window, and looking out, I saw the blurry image of a green courtyard with what appeared to be a banana tree in the middle. A hard rubber mattress without blankets lay on a metal bed frame that was bolted to the floor. It was a hell of a place to end up. I missed my funky room in the flophouse. It wasn't much, but spelled independence and freedom to me. It didn't look like I'd make it back there anytime soon.

Sleep eluded me. All I could do was mull over the series of small incidents that had added up to put me in that cell. It all started with the cash investment I gave to Johnny. Funny how it was exactly the amount he asked for, like a synchronicity of fateful numerology. My biggest mistake was not checking that I had enough money for rent before I left Johnny. Could I really trust him? Was there any truth to Carl's implication that I'd be gang banged by horny old men? I doubted that. After hanging out with Johnny for two weeks, he'd always been on the level with me. He'd come looking for me at the Girod Hotel in the morning, eager to share our profits. Too bad I never got the chance to see what Johnny's hustle was all about, and damn it, I missed my chance to get laid by a sexually experienced woman. When would I ever get a chance to taste some bearded clams and yodel in the canyon?

What a time for everything to fall apart in my new life. I wondered how Johnny would take the news that I'd been arrested. Maybe Frank would hand him the pile of my belongings, like he was my next of kin. I liked to think that he'd paste a black eye on Frank when he learned that his unbelievable stinginess had resulted in my arrest. Frank, along with Carl and the Monsignor, were the villains, and I hoped that the sanctimonious prig of a priest got what was coming to him. If Johnny was a Catholic, I hoped that cured him of it.

But what if Johnny's luck ran out too? Maybe he lost everything in that mysterious back room. Maybe he, too, wouldn't have his rent for Frank. He'd be out on his ass like me in this unforgiving world. But Johnny would land on his feet and damn it, so would I. There was nothing to do but carry on. I had to keep my chin up and deal with this situation. As a model prisoner, I'd have to bide my time and wait for another opportunity to escape.

32

THURSDAY, JUNE 8, 1967: JUVENILE LOCKDOWN

In the pre-dawn light, the blurred green image in the courtyard became clearer through the clouded Plexiglas. Finally, I recognized that it was indeed a banana tree, like I'd seen in books. Its lush green presence was a balm to my spirit, helping to calm me. I intended to stay strong, not to break down like the sniveling punk they said I was.

Bang! Bang! Bang! The muffled noise sounded far away, but steadily grew closer as a long progression of cell doors slammed open, one at a time. It was accompanied by indistinct male shouting. Then my sealed chamber barged open, and an angry looking black man peered in.

He shouted, "Get ready!" before he stopped with an amazed look on his face. "Well, I'll be. You're already up for the day, good. Five more minutes!" He slammed the door and was gone.

During what seemed more like twenty minutes, a swell of commotion arose outside. Young voices mixed with the banging doors. The black man popped in again and said, "Get up, get out!"

I sauntered out to join a line of prisoner boys assembling as our doors opened. Our keepers were all black men and almost all their charges were black, too. Out of the fifty or so inmates I saw, only four of us were white, but they were farther down the line from me, and quieter compared to the others. My black neighbors quizzed me.

"Hey white boy, what you in for? You kill anybody, white boy?"

"No, I just ran away from home."

"What the fuck? You is just a runaway? What's a runaway doing in a joint like this?"

They laughed. All of them claimed to be in for serious crimes, like armed robbery and burglary. A couple of young men, with massive adult muscles bulging through their short sleeves, were pointed out to me.

"They in for murder. Ya'all better be careful not to mess wit dem boys. They'd as soon kill you as look at you!" One of those muscular boys waved me over. "Hey white boy. Ya'all like dark meat? Ever fuck any black pussy, white boy?"

Answering that loaded question either way could get me in trouble. "No," I said.

He sneered at me. "What's the matter? Black pussy not good enough for you?"

"I never had the chance, man, but I'd sure like to try some."

That sent them all into delirious laughter.

"You want to taste that good black pussy. Don't you, white boy?"

They stuck their tongues through the V of their fingers and mimed the "yodeling in the canyon" technique, like Johnny had. They seemed friendlier now, clowning around as if the ice had been broken. Everything about me cracked them up. One pointed at my feet.

"White boy got crepe shoes! Do y'all wear crepe shoes up north, white boy?"

"I got them here."

They roared with laughter for reasons I could not fathom, because several of them wore the same kind of blue canvas shoes.

"Alright boys," the head counselor called out. "Form up and shut up-now!" He looked up and down the line with a fierce scowl. He was a big man and his charges responded, snapping to attention like soldiers. "You boys know the rules here. No talking, no pushing, touching, hands to yourselves or you will answer to me. Get that?"

A few other large black men, his underlings, positioned themselves strategically along the line. The head counselor then spoke into the intercom.

"Counselor number 10, coming through to dining hall." The door buzzed open, and he led us through a succession of doors that he buzzed to be opened in the same way. The doors slammed shut behind us. We were always between locked doors and under the vigilant gaze of muscular, no-nonsense men. This Juvenile detention was a maximum-security jail. After being marched through several doors along a series of long corridors, we at last reached the chow hall. We were not allowed to sit, but had to pass through several more arcane rites of passage. Counselors shouted orders.

"Hold out your hands!"

The silent line put out their right hands at a ninety-degree angle without a murmur. I copied them.

"Spoons!" A kitchen trustee in a white apron walked along the line, placing a spoon firmly in each of our hands as he counted. "One, two, three..."

"Forks!" This careful consignment was repeated until we held the two implements of a meal in our hands. These utensils looked and felt harmless. Made of a cheap alloy, they bent easily, rendering them almost useless as weapons.

Then we got our trays. They were segmented to keep our food separate. We passed through the chow line while business-like workers plopped a dollop of each of the several items offered onto our trays. We took our seats in the same shuffling assembly line order. Breakfast had the usual Southern staple grits, which I'd become accustomed to. Besides gray looking scrambled eggs, there was a new item I didn't recognize. It was a marbled brown and white sweet tasting food.

"What's this?" I said. "It's pretty good."

"White boy, don't you got no bread pudding where ya'all come from?"

The whole table laughed with him. One of them gave me his bread pudding, saying he was tired of it.

After eating, we lined up again. My new friends whispered to me to keep my utensils in hand rather than with the tray on the table. The head counselor called out: "Spoons!" We held out our spoons, going through the ritual of handing over our utensils one at a time. These were counted, handed over to another of the staff and tediously recounted until they were sure we'd surrendered every one. Only then did we march back through the maze of halls. Rather than put us back into our cells, we were taken to a bright dayroom.

The guys played cards or watched television. I finally met the white inmates, who had been farther down the line. They were more subdued than the blacks and spoke with less of an accent. Our counselors became more relaxed at this point, joking and chatting with their charges.

A dark-haired boy of about my age said, "We whites are like a species of exotic fish in this tank." He laughed at the comparison. "Just watch out for those bigger guys, man. They seem alright, but it's super easy to piss 'em off. If you do, they'll fuck you up bad."

He seemed like an easy-going, level-headed guy. I liked him at once.

"How did you get here?" I said.

"Oh, I didn't do anything violent, like some of those guys brag about." He motioned me over to an empty table beside a Plexiglas window with a hazy view of a green yard and tall fence. We got comfortable as he filled me in.

"My stepmother is a real bitch. Dad takes her side, of course. So I took the car and split for the weekend, staying at my buddy's place. Dad got all righteous, sicked the cops on me for car theft." He laughed. "Can you fucking believe it? Auto theft! Dad got me for borrowing the damn car."

He shook his head as if to clear it. "They've got a couple of other cars, including the Ferrari. It's not like they're ride-less. I've been here a week now. Shit, Dad says it'll do me good. Teach me a lesson." He laughed again, like it was all a big joke. "It isn't so bad here, man. I'm away from school and all their bullshit. I call this a vacation."

He wasn't interested in getting out of there. The other white guys had similar offenses. Like me, they were more about maladjustment, family and peer problems, with some shoplifting and a few fistfights thrown in.

"What's next?" I asked the dark-haired boy.

"They usually let us outside for baseball after lunch."

33

THE SHRINK

Minutes ticked away as slowly as hours. Lunch came at us like breakfast, marked by an obsessive counting of eating utensils. They fed us well, and I enjoyed the food. As we lined up to be let out into the barbed wire fenced yard, an attendant came with a clipboard and called my name.

"Schulz! You are to report to the psychologist's office. Follow me."

He led me along the halls to a colorful, pleasantly sunlit waiting room with normal glass windows that offered an unclouded view of the outside. It seemed out of place in this kid's jail.

"Make yourself comfortable and wait," he said, sounding friendlier in this environment. "It shouldn't be too long."

The room looked innocuous, a part of the free world. There were artsy pictures on the wall and colorful magazines laid out on a coffee table. After sitting alone for a few minutes, reading magazines to distract my mind, an office door opened. A pimple faced, strawberry blond girl of about my age emerged and the door closed behind her. For the first time, I realized that there must be a female section of this juvenile jail.

She sat beside me on the couch. "Hi. Are you here to see the shrink, too?"

"Yes, how did it go in there?"

"Don't worry. He only asks a bunch of dumb questions. My name's Jane." She extended her hand. "I'm a runaway, from Alexandria."

"I'm a runaway too, from Chicago."

"Really? Man, that's cool."

She told me she'd come down here to live with her uncle. "He's cool. Let me stay a week, but then he called my parents. Says I've got to go back home, eventually. I dunno." She sighed. "I'll probably have to run away again, because I hate it there."

I opened up to her. "I've been living on Skid row a couple of weeks. Maybe we both could bust out of here?"

She gazed at me for a moment, the wheels in her head spinning. "Maybe we could. After a few days, they let some of us girls out with an attendant. It would have been easy to slip away, pretending I had to go to the bathroom."

A door opened and a big, stern-faced black woman in a short Afro stepped in. "Let's go, Jane."

"Goodbye." She smiled and gave me a finger wriggling wave as they led her out. "Maybe I'll see you around?"

None of the magazines scattered around the waiting room distracted me. This lock-up appeared escape proof, but Jane told me that if I stayed a week or so, they might let me out under supervision. There could be a slim chance to escape and make it back to Johnny. The cops knew I'd been at the Girod Hotel and would look for me there. I'd have to find somewhere else, but I was broke, my chance of success slim. I told myself that I had to have faith, luck could change.

The office door opened, ending my reverie. A fellow in a white smock with a pleasant smile ushered me inside. He must be the shrink I'd been sent to see. After a brief *how do you do,* he gave me an inkblot and word association test. School psychologists put me through these tests back in Illinois.

"This interview is only a formality for our files," he said. "You will be released soon."

Relief shot through me. They must have realized that I was

innocent of any crime worth jail. Maybe I could get back to my life in New Orleans.

The shrink noticed my reaction and said, "Oh, didn't they tell you? Your parents are flying down from Chicago to fetch you. They'll arrive any moment."

That was a surprise. Airfare was expensive and my parents were cheapskates. I wasn't sure if it was good or bad news. They might ship me off to the Illinois Juvenile Detention Center in St. Charles, instead of bringing me home, and I wasn't sure which I preferred. My friend, Mike Filamoniak, had been there a year ago. It only held boys and was probably as tight as this facility.

The shrink said, "It's up to your parents and the local authorities what'll happen to you. Maybe they will put you into the juvenile court system, or maybe you'll just be sent home."

After all my effort to get free, I'd be back at my starting point, back to all the humiliation I'd fled, but at least the school year should be over for the summer.

The shrink touched on the legal aspects of my case. "Unless they found something more to hold you on, the police are required to cut you loose within seventy-two hours."

"What if I never gave them my correct name? Would I have been released?"

He chuckled. "Probably not. They would have found something to hold you on. You resisted an officer, which would be enough. You can't fight the system, son. Look at it this way; in a couple of years you can have your parents sign for you to join the Army."

At least I'd made it to New Orleans and managed to live on my own for a while. That experience boosted my self-confidence. I wasn't a loser, any more than anyone else. After all, everyone eventually loses at the game of life because we all end up dead. It is only a matter of when, so we might as well enjoy the journey no matter where it leads us. If I had to go back to Fenton, I wouldn't be the same as when I left. Fuck the bullies and the system that made them. I'd never surrender my spirit to be a bullied loser again.

34

PARENTAL CUSTODY

As we lined up for dinner, a councilor called my name and ushered me through the labyrinth of buzzing doors to the front office where two familiar strangers stood like mourners at a funeral. Dad was stone faced. Mom looked as if she'd been crying and reached out to me. I had to admit, her hug felt good.

She wiped away a tear. "How are you, Ronnie?"

"Fine, it's been a crazy day."

Dad shook my hand as if meeting me for the first time, without the harsh tongue lashing I expected. Despite everything, I cared about them. They were as flawed as any humans on the planet, but I knew they'd done their best. I loved them, but I couldn't tell them about my experiences, or explain the pressures, the humiliations building up in my life that forced me to leave. They gave me my life, and I owed them for my very existence, but not my future. That was up to me. My brain swirled with questions I couldn't ask. Would they send me to face charges and lock me away in St. Charles? I decided to play dumb, like some *Leave it to Beaver* stereotype of a clueless boy, spouting inane jabber.

"Gee, what time does the flight leave? Do you want to take a quick drive around New Orleans before we go to the airport?"

"No time for that," Dad said, his voice terse. "I've got to go to work in the morning."

He couldn't even take another day off work. Their lack of curiosity about this city that neither of them had seen before disappointed, but didn't surprise me. Maybe they worried that I'd try to get away, and yes, I toyed with the thought of losing them in the crowded airport. But it didn't seem right to slip away from them after they'd spent good money and Dad had taken a rare day off work. Anyway, I had no real chance of eluding the cops for long without money in my pocket. I'd bide my time and see how thing went.

We boarded a Delta Airlines direct flight to Chicago. This was my first time flying. There was only a slight elevator sensation on leaving the ground.

"It's almost like riding a bus," I said, trying to sound like a normal boy, not the oddball I seemed to them.

Mom cleared her throat. "Tomorrow is Friday, Ronnie, the last day of school. It's the finals, just a half day of testing and you'll come home."

"What the heck? I figured the school year would be over by now. It feels like I've been gone for ages."

When I tallied it up, I'd only been gone twenty-four days, an absence of just eighteen school days. In that time, I'd learned more of value than I ever could in algebra class. The weight that had hung on my shoulders before I left felt much lighter, giving me a new confidence that I'd be able to demand some respect no matter what they did to me.

My sisters looked at me like a stranger. The oldest, Darlene, finally spoke up. "Welcome home, Ronnie. After you left, the police searched your room, but they didn't do a very good job."

"Why is that, Dar?"

"They didn't find your map. The one you hid on your desk, with the route you traced to Montréal. As soon as the cops left, I went in to look around. And guess what? I found it and showed it to them! I could be a detective, you know."

That had been my deception plan, to throw them off my real

destination – New Orleans. The little snitch had long delighted in tormenting me, telling our friends embarrassing stories about me. Although closest to me in age, I never could confide in her, but this time, her snooping worked for me.

Sue, my next oldest sister, added some details. "They sent a cable to Montréal; they were looking for you up there. You sure pulled a fast one on them, but not fast enough, huh?"

35

FRIDAY, JUNE 9: FINALS AT FENTON

After my long absence, the classroom felt less threatening, more like the shadow of a distant nightmare. None of the teachers even questioned where I'd been. After sharpening my number two pencils, I took my seat and one by one, they passed out the tests. The stress that usually consumed me during tests didn't bother me at all. I took my time, indifferent to my grades, and filled in the bubbles on the multiple-choice questions and then turned them in to the stern-faced monitor. When I was done with them all, I left. In a couple of days, I would know the results.

It surprised me that my parents trusted me to come and go on my own, and I decided to enjoy the walk home along the railroad tracks instead of taking the school bus. The peaceful woods along the way soothed me. I missed my independent life in New Orleans, my partner Johnny, even my ramshackle room. Returning to my old *normal* happened so fast that it hadn't registered. Although I had freedom of movement, I was down to pennies in my pocket. Without cash, running away wouldn't be smart, but by the time summer ended, I hoped to have a new plan.

Mom's face was drawn tight when I stepped into the house. "Officer Sample came by while you were at school. You and I are going down to the Police Station to work out the details of your probation. You better have some lunch and get ready."

It was time for my punishment, to repay my debt to society. Maybe I'd get sent to St. Charles after all. The red brick police station was next to Salt Creek on Irving Park. It had been built just the year before, and shared half of the building with the village library. Officer Sample sat across the desk from Mom and me. He oversaw juvenile affairs, which accounted for most of the crime in this growing village, but unlike some of my friends, I didn't have a police record before I ran away, so he didn't know much about me.

His eyes glared at me, trying to intimidate me like the monsignor back in New Orleans. "We went to a lot of trouble over you, kid. We even sent circulars to Canada. You need to be taught a lesson you won't forget."

He looked at Mom. "Don't you agree?" She twisted in her seat and nodded. He turned back to me. "Your parents went through a lot of pain and heartache. This damn well better not happen ever again."

He leaned back in his chair, his eyes still boring into me as he relished his power as judge and jury to make me sweat before pronouncing the sentence. Although I was sure he'd already discussed punishment with my folks, I couldn't help feeling apprehensive.

"If it were up to me, you'd end up in St. Charles. But your parents are too easy on you, so you've got probation through the summer until school starts. You have to report to the police station twice a week, Tuesdays and Thursdays, for two hours of washing floors, cleaning toilets and what other tasks we come up with, all on an unpaid basis."

Dad came home from work after we got back, looking beat. Without a word, he went down into the basement after dinner but didn't take me with him. I was grateful for that.

To everyone's surprise, I got an "A" on the final exam in World

History, but due to my missed assignments, I ended up with a C for the year. Earth Science averaged out to a D, a passing score. It was no surprise that I failed Algebra, a class I could never stay awake in. Needing a mathematics prerequisite, I had to take General Math in summer school. I'd missed the Final for English One, which had taken place on the day before I got back. Listed as 'Incomplete,' I'd have to retake it again in my sophomore year at the same time as I began English Two classes. Too much English all at once and I didn't see a reason to care about the parts of speech.

36

SATURDAY, JUNE 10: GRANDPARENTS VISIT

Mom ran her fingers over her hair and gave me a cross look. "You know how hard this was on Grandpa, don't you? When he heard you ran away, he took off work and drove all along the highway, as far as the Mississippi River. You could have killed him, running off like you did."

Her words hit me hard. My knees felt weak, and I had to slump down at the kitchen table, where Mom had already set out the coffee cake. My leaving would hit him the hardest and I didn't want to hurt anyone, least of all my grandfather. We had a stronger bond than I felt with any other relative. He was sixty-four, still working, although a diehard smoker who suffered from Emphysema, which would kill him within five years. Although he had trouble catching his breath and had to climb the stairs two at a time before he had a bout of wheezing, he was still driving.

Grandpa understood me better than anyone. He ignored the deceptive map that Darlene, my detective sister, found and went by instinct. His searches along the highways of western Illinois had been close to the mark. If I hadn't been traveling by night, he might have found me.

Mom flipped the start switch on the coffee percolator. "He and

Grandma will be here soon. Comb your hair, wash your hands, and then put out the cups and saucers."

On Saturdays they always drove the twenty miles out from Chicago to us *in the country*, as Grandpa called the no longer rural town of Wood Dale.

Dad wasn't a conversationalist. It was hard for him to sit and socialize with anyone, so he usually came and went on his eternal projects around the house and yard. With company, especially her parents around, Mom was on her best behavior. She didn't whine, bitch, or slam doors like she usually did. A stranger could assume that she and Dad made a happy couple.

We got up when we heard the tan Buick pull into the driveway and held the screen door open. Mom met them with a shouted hello and a hug. For Grandma's sake, she began speaking louder than usual.

Grandma was a stingy, stubborn, third generation Bohemian German. "She'll squeeze a nickel until it squeaks," Grandpa always said. After a fever in her pre-teen years, she'd lost most of her hearing and continued using an early 1940s model hearing aid. She refused to let Mom get her a new one, despite numerous embarrassing incidents, misunderstanding store clerks and bus drivers.

"Don't waste the money," Grandma said. "I can hear just fine with this one." However, she did have a sense of humor, and even told ethnic jokes on herself. One went like this: "How do you take the census of a Bohemian neighborhood? Give up? You roll a nickel down the sidewalk; they'll all come running out for it."

"Howdy, Buck!" Grandpa greeted me as he usually did, with open arms and a bear hug. He didn't betray any of the anxiety Mom said he felt. Having me back, safe and sound, was enough for him.

"Ya know, Buck, I been thinking. There's things I've been meaning to do with you. Time sure flies. This summer, how's about we take us a trip down to see my side of the family? Just us men."

Mom set her coffee cup down with a clatter. "Dad, he can't go. He's on probation."

"Probation?" Grandpa grabbed the back of a chair and leaned

forward, wheezing. "What the Sam Hill for? All he did was run away. A boy's got to go off on his own sometimes. He didn't break no damn laws."

He heaved a few deep wheezing breaths before continuing. "I run away too when I was his age. Went to Texas and Oklahoma, driving mules and chasing cattle. Did I ever tell you how I helped build the very first paved highway in Texas?"

Mom put her hand on his shoulder. "Sit down Dad. The doctor said for you to take it easy. Have some coffee and cake."

He sat beside Grandma, who had already cut him a piece of cake. He had to take a few more wheezing breaths before resuming. "How the hell's a boy supposed to grow into a man, if he can't run off and figure his-self out?"

"Well, Dad, things are different now."

"I guess they is." Grandpa looked down at his hands, which were brown and leathery, his fingernails so hard that he trimmed them with his pocketknife. He looked so dejected that Grandma, normally distant, put her arm around him.

"It'll just have to wait 'til after summer school," Mom said. "It ends July 28; you can take him then."

Mom walked to the banister and called upstairs. "Girls, come down. Grandma and Grandpa are here!"

My five younger sisters clomped downstairs. Grandpa opened his arms wide for a hug. "Gimme some sugar, girls." He collected a smooch from each of them before sitting down.

Grandma had already cut their coffeecake and was setting it out on plates around the table. I poured myself a coffee and joined them. We didn't talk about my situation at the table with the girls around, keeping it light. Afterwards I joined Grandpa on our usual stroll around the *back forty* of our single acre back yard.

"Them strawberries is coming in real good." Grandpa carefully bent over the row, picked a few and popped one in his mouth. "Nice and sweet. Try one. Corn is coming in too."

In years past, Grandpa had enjoyed working the garden on the weekends. He'd let me sit on his lap and steer the medium-sized Ford tractor when I was little. I enjoyed working with him. Unlike Dad, he was easy-going, never upset if I didn't do things perfectly.

We rounded back through the apple trees. Grandpa sat on the long stack of bricks behind the garage. As he caught his breath, he noticed something. "What's that on your wrist?" He sounded concerned.

"Oh, that's my souvenir from the New Orleans cops." A deep red indented mark remained over my wrist bone where the tight handcuff had dug deep into it. Grandpa was the only one to have noticed it. He grew angry.

"Them bastards. They had no right to treat you that way. What else did they do?"

"They kicked me around and punched me after I'd tried to get away from them."

"That don't give 'em the right to beat you. Ya know, Buck, you're my only grandson, my pride and joy. Your dad don't know what the hell to do with you." He chuckled and grabbed my shoulder, looking me over. "I suppose you take more after my side, rather than those *square-head Krauts* on his side of the family." We both laughed. It seemed true. "You'll be on your own soon enough. I just want you to hang in there another year or so. At least you got-ta keep the cops off your back."

What could I say? I nodded in affirmation.

"We put this trip to southern Illinois off way too long, Buck. You ain't never met any of my people. I called my brother, Marcus. He's out in Liberty, Missouri. My other brothers is long dead. He'll come, might be the last I see him too. Life is too short to wait any longer." He let out a long sigh, as if setting down a heavy load. Grandpa knew his days were numbered. Soon he wouldn't be able to get around. Mom told me the guys at work covered for him, giving him straw boss jobs that let him feel useful without doing much. He joked it was practically welfare.

On Tuesday, I started my cleanup duties at the Cop shop, as we called the police station. Officer Sample pointed me to the janitor's closet, where I got the broom and mop. I emptied the wastepaper baskets, scrubbed the sink and toilet, and mopped the floor. The station was small, shared with the village library that took half of the oblong building, so mopping the floor didn't take long, and the cops didn't ride my ass like Dad did. They never told me to redo a job, and even complimented me on a job well done, something Dad never did. I wasn't a lazy slouch and took pride in my work. They knew about my upcoming trip with Grandpa, which excused me for a week until I got back. All in all, it wasn't too bad of a deal.

∗

37

THE LONG HOT SUMMER

A ngry black teenagers faced the bayonets of soldiers. Red blood streamed across the pavement. A cop brandishing a shotgun stood over the young black boy who lay motionless on the street. Thick smoke curled above blocks of buildings; the streets covered in broken glass. Helicopters buzzed high over truck convoys full of helmeted men. Those television images seared my brain. I was used to scenes from the Vietnam War, but this wasn't Vietnam. These were scenes of war in American cities. Full-on Race war seemed inevitable as I watched and read the stories and speeches by government officials and radical leaders.

June 1967 was the beginning of a long, hot summer of racial turmoil. As I prepared to travel with Grandpa to discover my roots, ghettos exploded across the nation and the death toll rose. It felt like we were going on a voyage into America's heart of darkness. My sympathies lay with the rioters, but my family and neighbors wanted them crushed and put back in their place. How could I reconcile these people, *my* people, who'd brought me into this world and wanted to mold me into an adult like them, while every part of me wanted to resist and fight back against their influence.

"When you're older, you'll understand," they insisted. In a few years, they assured me, I'd become more like my father, an unquestioning conservative who only wanted his piece of the pie, a comfortable place in the status quo, not changes to the social order that benefited the disenfranchised, who were, they claimed, only lazy, shiftless bums. Was I destined to become like them? Hell no! I had to be true to my conscience, which I'd hidden deep within my heart.

There were two sides to my family, the American and the German. Dad's mom was born in Germany. She'd come here with her family at the age of nine, and in 1920 she married my other grandpa, a second-generation German. That's all I knew about them at the time; they both died before I was eight years old. It flabbergasted me that Dad and his brother didn't know where in Germany their mom or grandparents were born. They weren't even curious, fobbing off my questions with careless, *I dunno,* shrugs. Genealogy intrigued me, but that was something rich people with time on their hands did. With so little information, I had no idea how to trace my family tree.

My only surviving grandpa, Ernie, represented my American side, even though he'd married Alice, a third-generation Bohemian-German girl, who'd grown up speaking English as a second language in Wisconsin. Technically, that made me three-quarters German. Grandma Alice wouldn't tell us much about her family, but she could rattle off the Ten Commandments and alphabet in German. There were horrible scandals, including suicides and a murder she wanted to hide. All of that I only discovered years later, when I had the time to dig into it. My German identity, which was marred by two World Wars' worth of atrocities, was a big mystery that I knew nothing about.

Grandpa Ernie claimed we were part Native American on his side. Intrigued, I had to learn more, and he wouldn't live forever. Taking this trip to southern Illinois was something we'd mulled over for years while he grew older, and his emphysema worsened. For his sake, I promised that I'd stick around another year before trying to leave home again.

38

ON THE ROAD AGAIN

S ummer School ended Friday, July 28, 1967. The next day, Grandpa pulled into our driveway in his tan Buick.

"We need to get us some white gas for the camp stove," he said as I hopped into the front seat beside him. I supposed it was something like kerosene. We stopped at a shabby establishment by the corner of Addison and Lake Street. Noxious fumes assailed my nose as we filled his big banged up red can that had seen decades of use. Grandpa knew the old man who ran the shop.

"This here's my grandson," he said, thumping my shoulder.

I shrugged off my embarrassment, but not too forcefully. It felt good to be loved by the old man. This would be our first and last long outing together.

"We'll be camping our way to southern Illinois to see what's left of my people down there."

"Oh, yeah?" the man said. "Where exactly?"

"I was born on a farm near Grafton. Nobody's left there now. We'll drive on down to Alton, where some of my cousins are. My brother Marcus is coming up from Kansas City to meet us. Ain't seen him in a long spell."

I listened with interest. After he and his brothers were adopted by different families in 1909, it took them thirty-two years to find each other. Grandpa had shown me newspaper articles from January 1942. Weeks after the Japanese bombed Pearl Harbor; they reunited in St. Louis. Despite the war on the front pages, the reunion of lost brothers made for a human-interest story in the local papers.

We dropped the full can of gas in the trunk and headed out. The Chicago suburbs gave way to green fields in open country. We followed Route 53 south to Joliet, then west along the Illinois River on two-lane roads. The intricate labyrinth of expressways wouldn't cover the area and block out the rural scenery until a couple of years later.

As he drove, Grandpa pointed out landmarks and talked about some of the towns he'd worked in, moving heavy machinery and monuments, statues and gravestones. Then he got back to his family, telling me about the shock of being separated from his mother and three brothers as a child after their stepfather's suicide. The youngest, Everett, hadn't even known of his adoption until he needed his birth certificate, so he could register for a Social Security card. He was married with two kids of his own by the time they found him. Even though I was eager to know more, I didn't say anything that could interrupt his story.

"You see, Buck, Everett's wife was scandalized by our Ma, your great grandma. Said she was a wanton woman who dumped her kids in an orphanage, so she could carry-on with men." He half turned to look at me, eyes wide as he feigned the woman's self-righteous shock, then he chuckled, like it was a joke. He drove in silence for a while, coughed, and continued. "Well, true enough, Ma took up with the wrong kind of men, they was all scrappers and bootleggers, runnen illegal moonshine even before 1920, when national prohibition came in. Everett's wife never even let her kids meet their grandma, told 'em she was dead and buried, instead of living just a few blocks away from them in St. Louis."

Tired of talking, he switched on the radio.

President Johnson ordered paratroopers from the 82nd Airborne onto the streets of a paralyzed Detroit joining thousands of National Guard troops... President Johnson has established a Commission to investigate the cause of the rioting...

Violence raged across the country. In all, 159 race riots erupted in the United States that summer. Atlanta, Boston, Cincinnati, Buffalo, Minneapolis, and the list went on. Newark and Detroit were the deadliest. We listened in silence. Grandpa seemed to be searching for words.

"Now, Buck." He nodded his head, with a voice as measured and gentle as when he'd spoken to me as a toddler. "These riots..." He took a breath. "There's things you just gotta accept about how this here world works. Negroes has got to live among their own kind. They don't know how to keep their neighborhoods clean and orderly as white folks do. Agitators rile 'em up, make 'em expect what they can't have."

He took a few breaths again as he saw an opportunity and passed another car. He hated driving behind road hogs and Sunday drivers, as he called them.

"Well, Buck, those colored people are like children. They need to learn good work ethics and to pick up after themselves, like us white folks do."

Grandpa saw no contradiction between segregation for blacks and his pride over his sliver of Native American heritage, even though Indian Reservations that I'd seen myself up in Wisconsin were as impoverished and dilapidated as urban ghettoes. That was different somehow. Balancing my love for the old man while sidestepping his hateful opinions was a complicated layer of my life, but what he said next caught me off guard.

"Now, Buck, you listen to what that Ku Klux Klan has to say. They got a point, you know. Just keep an open mind, hear 'em out, is all I'm askin."

This was the first time I'd heard Grandpa mention the KKK, let alone in a favorable light. Was my loving, silken voiced grandfather a secret Klan member? From my reading, I knew the Klan was against Native Americans too, as well as Catholics and Jews, sometimes even Italians. Grandpa read the papers and had to be as aware of that as I was. It didn't make sense, but I knew by then that bigotry wasn't rational or limited to just one ethnic group.

I'd read about the "Civilized Tribes" of Native Americans, the Cherokee, Chickasaw, Choctaw and Seminole survivors of the Trail of Tears, who'd been force marched from their ancient homelands to Oklahoma. Many of them, being "civilized" plantation owners by that time, also owned black slaves who came west with them. Despite their grievances or experience with intolerance, many of these *Indians* later fought for the Confederacy, even against their own tribesmen who remained loyal to the Union. Oklahoma was Indian Territory and became a bloody battleground in the Civil War, a chapter that we never read about in high school history class. The thought of American Indian racists was counter-intuitive. It didn't seem logical, but I was learning more from my experience than in a dry classroom about how crazy humans could be.

What sort of people were those unmet relatives of mine? Grandpa always said family was important to him. Why had it had taken so long for me to meet any of them? None of my sisters ever did.

A terrifying idea exploded in my head. Maybe Grandpa intended to recruit me into the Klan. The thought shocked me, but I needed to understand how he came to his conclusions, which seemed abhorrent to me. Like a secret agent in enemy country, I'd keep my cool and scope this out. Grandpa's racism seemed to have deep roots. I wondered if his ancestors were slave owners, overseers, or passive participants in those crimes.

The Ku Klux Klan had begun in the south after the Civil War to prevent blacks from voting or organizing to receive better wages. It could be said that the slave owners lost the War, but they won the peace, as Jim Crow restrictions and Klan terror recreated near slavery conditions for blacks in the south. Many went north to work in the growing industrial cities, like Chicago and Detroit, but here too, they were forced to live in restricted areas, ghettos, and got less pay for the same work as whites.

Grandpa came to Chicago too, in 1925, looking for the same advantages and felt entitled to his piece of the pie, which disappeared in the Great Depression five years later. Maybe he felt there wasn't enough pie to go around in the scramble for jobs if blacks got equal pay.

Sensing my unease, Grandpa pointed as the broad river came into view. "The Illinois River figures big in our family story. My pa drowned in it back in 1907." He hesitated, shifting his hands on the steering wheel as he weighed his words and perhaps his emotions. "I told you that already, but I didn't tell you it was no accident. He drowned his-self, and I stood on the riverbank and watched him go."

With that, he had my full attention.

"Ma already had three boys and was expecting another with her new husband, my stepfather, the only pa I remembered. Pa came home drunk, yellen' about how he was gonna kill his-self. Ma didn't pay him no mind. He always talked like that when he was drunk. Us boys followed him down to the river. It wasn't far behind the house. He waded in until his broad-brimmed hat floated away as he went under. The oldest, John, went in and fetched the hat, sent little Marcus to call a neighbor for help while we stayed and watched for him, but Pa never came back up."

We rode in silence for a while as I considered what would have driven this man to suicide. He'd married a woman who already had three boys and was expecting another – his own son. Grandpa told me they couldn't pay the mortgage on the farm. The Ontis family had owned it since the 1850s, but times were tough and money was scare. They were about to be dispossessed. Farming was all his stepdad knew, and his prospects must have appeared hopeless, but I had another burning question that nagged at me. "What about our Indian blood?"

Grandpa cleared his throat. "My ma's side was French Canadian Indian. My Great-Grandma Sophia was bronze colored, like an Indian, darker than the French people who raised her and they was half-breeds."

Grandpa had told me that for years, but he didn't know any more about it. It was left to me, years later, to dig into our past with the help of DNA. His great-grandma Sophia was the midwife who delivered him into this world. She had to have been a full Native American for so much a percentage of that DNA to come down to my generation. Census records said he was born in Iowa in 1832, when the only whites allowed in Iowa were French Canadian Indian traders, and she was possibly an orphan of the Black Hawk War, which occurred that year.

The tribes were forced to move from Illinois to Iowa west of the Mississippi, but that only lasted until the Americans wanted Iowa too. Indian removal was the order of the day, because they stood in the way of white America's Manifest Destiny, and government policy supported land hungry American citizens.

Reading local histories, I found details about the Indian trade in the Mississippi valley, along with plenty of disparaging remarks about half-breeds. Racism was rife in the nineteenth century. From Tom Sawyer's Injun Joe on down, they were cast as amoral villains, embodying the worst of both peoples. Those who could, passed for white, just as many white-black mixed mulattoes did. They hid their genetic history as best they could and their descendants often fell into a black hole, ignorant of their true history. Some, without a doubt, became Klan supporters.

Sophia would not have been welcomed into proper white society, but the clan of poor white farmers she married into in the decade before the Civil War lived in the *hills and hollers* of Jersey County, Illinois, and were anything but proper. Poor as they were, they ranked higher than the slaves across the Mississippi River in Missouri. Slave catchers searched the nearby woods for runaway black slaves. Our ancestors may even have joined in the search, like their neighbors did, to turn in escaped slaves for the reward.

39

ALONG THE ILLINOIS RIVER

W e came to a wide parking area along the river side of the road to stretch our legs. A black woman with three young boys stood on giant rocks piled along the river, fishing with homemade poles. I watched with apprehension as Grandpa walked up to them. He tussled the woolly hair of the youngest.

"Boy, how's the fishen today? Catch anything?" His voice was friendly, relaxed, which surprised me after his lecture on segregation.

The older boy pointed to a bucket. "We got a few big enough to eat."

Inside I saw catfish and carp. Grandpa usually called carp trash fish and bottom feeders, but today he was diplomatic.

"Them's good eaten. You boys like to fish? I done plenty of that. Used to live along this river a fair piece south of here."

"They love to fish," their mother said, giving Grandpa a broad smile. "Helps me fill the dinner table." She was an exceptionally pretty, well-proportioned woman in her mid-twenties. Even a racist would have to agree. Her pure white teeth stood out against her smooth, coal-black skin.

Grandpa smiled back and came close to her. "You got yourself some fine boys. I reckon they'll be the men of the house someday."

This was the first time I'd seen Grandpa interact with black people. His friendliness was a relief, but I could still hear his earlier words ringing in my head. I'd been thinking a lot about hypocrisy and double standards. Racism had always struck me as not only cruel, but irrational. The racists I knew treated all manner of slavering dogs as family, while fearing to sit with, or drink from the same water fountain as black humans.

I came to understand it was just fear turning into hate, fear of losing their small slice of superior prestige to another group of people. DNA has finally proven how all of us, no matter our skin color, descend from a small family group in Africa thousands of years ago. All our differences in appearance are only adaptations to the continually changing environment.

As they chatted like old friends, Grandpa seemed to be flirting with the woman. I hid my amazement, deciding I wouldn't interfere if he did. Crossing the color line so intimately could help change his prejudice. Maybe, if I weren't standing right next to him, he would make a move on this lady. He told her all about our trip while standing within inches of her. Finally, he let out a deep sigh and turned to me.

"Well, Buck, I suppose we ought to hit the road, find us a campsite before dark."

He gave the boys a fond last pat on the head as they smiled up at him. Before we reached the car, the woman waved and called out, "It was sure nice meeting you fellas."

Grandpa smiled at her, then back to me as he slid into his side. "She's a good looken gal, ain't she, Buck?"

I nodded agreement. I wanted to ask how segregation jibed with his obvious pleasure in her company but was unsure how to phrase it. Better to let him do the talking.

"You know, Buck, there's good Negroes and then there's just plain *niggers*."

Yes, I'd heard that from him many times.

"Now, I work with a real nice colored man, name of Clyde. He's very respectful, does his job and don't cause no trouble." This was the code I knew. Trouble meant saying anything that questioned the pervasive racism reflected in the status quo. "We play cards together after work and he agrees with me. Negroes has got no business living in the same neighborhood as white folks. We both need to be among our own kind, is all."

Clyde probably knew better than to risk his job by appearing an *uppity* troublemaker to his white coworkers. I wondered what his honest thoughts were about segregation and Grandpa.

Grandpa was a soft-hearted racist, but that's what he was, a product of his times. I wanted to go easy on him, like Clyde apparently did, but I couldn't agree with him.

Pulling into a State Park, we lit up the Coleman stove to heat stew and cocoa before pulling out blankets and sleeping in the car, he in the front, and me in the backseat. Next morning it was eggs, bacon and we got back on the secondary roads through progressively steeper rolling hills with little traffic.

40

MY UNKNOWN KINFOLK

It was still morning when we came to a sharp curve. It was a quarter mile past a little red church and cemetery where Grandpa said his "people" were buried. He pulled onto the shoulder and stepped out. A sunken lane ran due south through cornfields to a tree line two hundred yards away. Without a word, Grandpa stood gazing along the rutted lane for some time. Standing beside him, I saw tears welling up in his eyes, which he tried to hide from me.

"There was a clapboard covered log cabin halfway across that field." He stifled a cough. "That's where I was born. The river lay right behind those trees. When Pa drowned, the mortgage was foreclosed, times was tough for everyone. When none of her brothers could take us in, Ma put us kids in the orphanage and my family fell apart." Turning away, so I couldn't see the tears on his face, Grandpa went back around to the driver's side.

Passing through the next town of Grafton, he said, "My family lived around here about a hundred years. Sure hasn't changed that much." He didn't say more in answer to my questions, and we rode in silence the rest of the way to Alton. We pulled up to a white frame house and got out.

A gray, still buxom old woman at the door beamed at us. "Well, I'll be. This must be that grandson you're always bragging about." She gave him a big hug, then me.

"Buck, this is yer aunt Edna."

She smiled and said, "Marcus got here ahead of y'all. He's around back." She led the way through the house.

The thin old man rose from a lawn chair to meet us. His white hair was parted straight down the middle, reminding me of nineteenth century barkeeps in movies.

"Well, howdy, Bud." He greeted Grandpa with a shaky handshake. "Been a coon's age since we saw you. You brought the boy, I see." He smiled at me. "About time we saw him, 'cause we ain't getten any younger."

"Buck," Grandpa said. "This is yer Uncle Marcus." He gestured to another woman who joined us. "That's Lyda, Marcus's wife."

It seemed all of them only knew me as Buck. They called Grandpa Bud. The first time I'd heard that nickname for him. Long after he passed away, I found some old letters addressed to him as Bud.

Several more people showed up. One of them stood out. He was about Grandpa's age, mid-sixties, and over six feet tall like him. He skewered me with a nasty glower, as if he wanted to pick a fight. Then he shot out his right hand and grabbed mine, startling me.

"So, you're Buck? I heard a lot about you." His eyes narrowed even more, as if he didn't like what he saw. I swallowed a wave of panic as I wondered what he'd heard. Was I about to be hazed or initiated into a Klan chapter?

"I'm the goddamn fighting Irishman," he said as he slugged my shoulder with his left, hard, while still holding my right in a visor grip. "You worried your grandpa sick running off to New Orleans. What the hell for? He's too soft on you. I'd a walloped you a good one." He slugged me again, even harder, before releasing my hand.

Grandpa laughed. "Don't pay him no mind, Buck." He coughed, and then leaned forward on the table to catch his breath. "Irish and I are still trying to figure out if we're half-brothers. You see, his pa may be mine too, by a different ma. It all depends on which story is true."

Grandpa and Irish had a stronger resemblance than Marcus, who was shorter and didn't look like either one.

Lyda brought two big watermelons, and we sliced and ate until the six o'clock news came on the television, which they'd brought outside, attached to a long extension cord. We were bombarded with an avalanche of updates on the riots. It had simmered down to tense community negotiations and recrimination over who was responsible for the brutality. Irish slammed his fist on the table, bouncing our glasses of lemonade.

"Goddamn Niggers is runnen wild all over this country. Shoot 'em when they loot, I say! Bet that'll quiet things down real fast." They all used the word "Nigger," unselfconsciously, in a neutral tone of voice, but his tone was venomous.

"Oh, settle down there, Irish." Marcus's gentle voice tried to soothe him. "They got a Nigger Deputy Sheriff down in Cairo, you know. He keeps his people in line, clubs 'em upside the head if they don't listen. I respect how he handles things. Those riots coulda been a lot worse down there, ya know."

Over the next day and a half, I gleaned what I could about these people I was related to. The subject of the Klan didn't come up, and I felt relieved about that. I'd grown up in a different world from theirs. Grandpa's birth family had remained in southern Illinois and Missouri. In running away from his adoptive family, he'd escaped that orbit. He'd wandered through every state but Hawaii until he found work in Chicago. Then he got a wife, a daughter and then came us grandkids, tying him more to us in Chicago than to his birth family, but he still carried his prejudice with him.

It was up to me and my generation to end that poisonous tradition. Maybe our children and their children's children would have to continue the fight long into the future. In my lifetime, I've seen progress, but at times our gains seem to vanish as our culture slips backward into intolerance.

Homeward bound, we crossed to Missouri and drove north along the Mississippi River. Grandpa pointed to a sign for the hamlet of Sulfur Springs.

"After I got adopted out of the orphanage, I grew up on a farm near here. Stingy, Bible thumping people they was." He began to get agitated, banging his hands on the steering wheel. "The old man was a deacon in the church. They worked me like a damn mule! I could never call that woman Ma. Their hired man always got a much bigger dish of scotch pudding than I did, and seconds too! It was my favorite, but they only gave me a small dish of it."

He locked eyes with mine, as if to convey a deeper understanding of the injustice. "I knew why you had to run away too, Buck. You're so much like me. If I hadn't run, I might have killed 'em."

I burned with curiosity for more details. "Show me where the old place was."

"They're all dead now, nothing to see," he said, stepping on the gas, roaring away from his memories and the answers to my questions.

We camped outside Hannibal, Missouri, by the cave made famous by Mark Twain's book, Tom Sawyer. That's where the much-maligned Injun Joe died in the story. Mark Twain seemed to be the author best suited to explain our family background, and I knew nothing of any others who wrote about those river people who may have been related to my ancestors.

In the morning, I took the cave tour, something I'd always wanted to do. Grandpa wasn't interested in going, but it did not disappoint me. There were miles of passages. Some, the guide said, were still unexplored. They stretched in a complex underground maze. It was easy to get lost forever if you weren't careful. The guide said they went under the Mississippi as far as Illinois. Dogs from Illinois, unlikely to have swum across the broad Mississippi, had turned up on that side.

Many interesting stories besides Twain's had taken place there. There was the doctor who kept his deceased young daughter preserved in one passage, hoping to find a cure for death and bring her back to life. The usual tales of bandit loot and hidden

Confederate gold added to the allure of the place. Wandering through the long tour I wondered if the half-breed Injun Joe was based on a real person. He might be related to our side of the family, and I felt a lot of sympathy for him.

Coming back, I found Grandpa suddenly anxious to get back to Chicago. By that evening he'd driven us straight back, stopping only for gas and to fix the car's malfunctioning water pump. As we rode along in silence, I had a lot to ruminate on. The issues of a century ago, prejudice and injustice, were still relevant, and I felt connected to the ongoing history. It was my story too, and we were all connected in this never-ending pageant.

The branching tree of our family connected the orphaned Native American girl, Sophia, from Iowa to Missouri and to the small farm on the banks of the Illinois River, where she bore thirteen children. Beyond Sophia and her American husband stretched a line of more ancient, unknown ancestors, Native American and European, all refugees from wars and economic disasters. The more I learned about them all, the more I understood what drove them in their turbulent times, times much like our own, because people hadn't changed as much as the technology to kill and control each other had.

We tend to idolize our ancestors, seeing them as better, stronger, braver than we are, but I'd come to see them for who they were, like my grandpa, human products of their times. He'd run away from a sort of slavery to his adoptive parents, but he couldn't see the connection between his situation and the larger issues of economic abuse and racial intolerance all around him. We shared a bond despite everything, and I couldn't help loving the old man.

41

HIGH ON MARS

Stripping off my shirt, I stepped into a blazing afternoon. I'd worked up a sweat at the police station performing my probation appointed jobs. It was time to pay my pal Paul a visit and fill him in on my exploits. His dad, Mr. Ladendorf, stood under the hood of his car in the driveway and straightened up as I approached.

"Well, look what the cat dragged in!" he shouted. "We were wondering what became of you, young man." He looked up at the house. "Paul! Come see who's here."

Paul and I became fast friends after he was kicked out of Holy Ghost Catholic School and came to my eighth-grade class in public school. He and the nearby Diezel brothers were lovers of the woods like me. He came out with his younger brother Mark and gave me a bear hug. Mark yanked my neck down to his shorter size and loudly kissed my sweaty back. His enthusiasm surprised me.

"What's with the kiss?"

He laughed. "That's how my biker pals greet each other. It's a brotherhood thing, doesn't mean we're queer or anything."

What little Mark hanging around biker gangs? That surprised me as much as the kiss. Paul's tolerant smile told me he had accepted his younger brother into our company.

Mr. Ladendorf shrugged and turned back to his engine. It was all beyond him, but I thought his style of parenting was less intrusive than Dad's, which is why we always hung out at Paul's house rather than mine.

"Chopper introduced me to some of the Chicago Outlaws," Mark said. "They're alright guys." Chopper got his nickname long before he was into cycle gangs, who called their bikes choppers or hogs. His lower jaw protruded an inch or two beyond his upper teeth, reminding me of a Dick Tracy comic strip character.

Paul and Mark were fast becoming greasers. Even though, like me, they admired the growing hippie phenomenon. We had to create our own way, because the only game in town was the tough greaser culture.

"What do you think about hip greasers?" I asked.

"Yeah, like I dig it!" Mark said.

"Seriously, man, greasers are just working-class guys, like us. We're all rebels against the establishment," Paul said.

Taking such a philosophical view made me feel better about blurring the line between the social cliques of high school. Baggy gray pants and nylon shirts were standard attire for greasers. The only tangible souvenirs that I'd brought back from New Orleans were the angry red scar on my wrist and Tom's baggy gray pants I happened to be wearing. I'd lost most of my clothes on the sidewalk back in New Orleans, and much as I hated to, I would have to prevail upon Mom to buy me some nylon shirts.

Paul snapped his fingers. "Hey Ron, I'd better tell you about some bad shit that happened since you've been gone. Remember Cheetah?"

"You mean Tarzan's chimp?"

"No, but close. He was a guy I introduced you to last year. Everyone picked on him. His real name is Ed Viens, but everybody called him Cheetah because when he got excited or angry he'd jump up and down screeching like Tarzan's Chimp."

On August first, soon after Grandpa and I left on our trip, six-year-old Kevin Carnow went missing and sixteen-year-old Ed Viens volunteered to help his neighbors search the fields for him. He walked far ahead of the others and was the one who found the boy's strangled body. His helpful, yet morbid interest in the case made him a suspect and, under questioning, he confessed and was charged with the murder.

The Viens family had just moved to Bensenville from Boston. His Mother was divorced, new in town and working long hours to support her three kids. The *cool* crowd of boys tormented Ed, who they called Cheetah, without mercy. They said he was a retard, and he acted strange. His tormentors poured sticky liquids into his locker almost every day and they pushed him around and mocked him, especially in gym class. The gym teachers did nothing about it. It was survival of the fittest at Fenton, and a boy had to fight his own battles or be mocked as a wimp.

The cool guys would be at a party. "Let's call Cheetah's house!" someone said just to harass and make fun of him. His Mother would grab the phone and beg them. "Please stop. Why are you calling him all those names?"

A few kids, like Paul, did try to stand up for him, but the tough guys would say, "Hey, he's Cheetah Monkey, do you want some of his trouble too?" and the bravest defenders chickened out, leaving Ed friendless and alone, but as he was suffering, he bullied other kids smaller than him, including the neighborhood girls. Then he'd done the unthinkable and made himself notorious by strangling a six-year-old boy.

Before I ran away, I'd been at my wit's end and suicide had been on my mind as a kinder, more socially responsible solution to my problems than murdering an innocent creature. Most of us think we could never sink so low, that there was no excuse for the murder of a child, but in an environment of unrelenting emotional abuse, everyone has a breaking point, an irrational dark side, that we, as a society, need to better understand if we are to stop turning out misfits.

———

Paul started quizzing me. "So, where ya been all this time? I heard you ran away to New Orleans. Is it true?"

Mark broke in. "He can tell us on the way, because you're here just in time, Ron."

"In time for what?"

"It's a surprise," Paul said, walking backwards with a sideways glance at his dad, so I knew not to ask for clarification. "Let's get going."

Beyond their dad's earshot, Mark winked. "Should I tell him?"

"Tell me what? Where are we going?"

"Mark has a dude he wants us to meet."

As we walked east along busy Irving Park Road, I gave a condensed version of my experiences in New Orleans.

"Well, I'm glad you're back, man," Mark said.

"Me too," Paul said with a big grin. He nudged Mark, who took over.

"This guy, Bob Mars, lives right across Irving Park from... What was that restaurant you worked at?"

"Ehlan's Green Tree Inn."

"Yeah, the Green Tree Inn. Thinking about getting your job back?"

"I don't think so. Mom told me Mr. Ehlan is upset with me for leaving without notice. How could I? I was running away! It's too embarrassing to beg him for the job back. So, tell me. What's this Bob into?"

"Bob is cool," Mark said. "He's new in town, but he's totally out of shape and will never make a Woods Runner like us."

By that time, we stood before a two-story, white frame house. Mark led the way up the steps to the front door and rang the bell.

"Hey, Bob," Mark greeted the guy who opened the door.

Bob eyed me with suspicion. "Who're these guys?"

"This is my bro, Paul, and his buddy Ron. They're cool. Ron ran away to New Orleans and just got back. You got the stuff?"

Bob Mars was as short as Mark. His hair was jet black and over his ears. It would never pass Fenton's dress code in the fall and he would have to cut it. We trooped upstairs to his bedroom. The brothers sat on the bed; I squatted on the rug beside Bob. He opened a plastic baggie and took out some green shredded flakes. It looked like parsley but had a pungent, earthy smell. He put some on a sheet of rolling paper and proceeded to roll and light the first joint I'd seen.

"You ever smoke pot before?" Bob asked me. "Must have had some good shit down in New Orleans, huh?"

"No, never saw it. All I had was wine and beer. I heard there was heroin around, not that I'd ever try that. Is it true that pot is addictive and leads to heroin?"

"Naw, it ain't nothing like heroin. In fact, it's not bad for you like booze, and it is mind expanding. You've got to inhale and hold it as long as you can before letting it out." He demonstrated the technique and handed the joint to me. I filled my lungs with smoke. "Now pass the joint around." I slowly let out my breath and passed the joint to Mark.

The joint soon came full circle. Bob wheezed as he handed it to me. "Have another hit." As I took it, he exhaled a slow, languorous curl of smoke that formed an "O" and floated to the ceiling. After another round, Mark exhaled his own long curl of smoke and flopped back on the bed, saying, "Wow, man, I'm stoned." He started rolling around on the bed, and making weird faces.

Paul was unaffected. "Knock it off, Mark," he said, but his brother kept lolling about.

Other than some expected mild dizziness from holding my breath, the pot had no effect on me. I turned to Bob. "He's joking, right? I don't feel a thing."

"No," he said gravely to Paul and I. "Mark doesn't know what he's doing; he's stoned out of his head."

"There are other ways to get high," I said. "I've been reading books on Yoga and Hindu mysticism."

Bob and Paul looked interested, so I continued while Mark rolled around in his own world.

"I've been practicing *Pranayama* breath control. That's the ticket for me. Gives me a floating sensation, like I'm leaving my body. It gets me higher than this pot. Already I feel like I'm opening my third eye."

"My dad meditates," Bob said.

"Your dad?" That floored me. My dad thought it was cuckoo. Most of that generation seemed disinterested in finding the truth behind ordinary reality. Bob's dad *had* to be cool.

Bob nodded. "Yeah, he smokes pot with me sometimes. He fought in the British Army in North Africa during the war. He'll be home soon. He could give you meditation lessons."

Bob didn't jump up and hide his stash, like I would have, when we heard his dad come in the house and climb the stairs.

Mr. Mars knocked on the door. "Everything all right in there?" Unlike Bob, he had a distinctive British accent.

"Sure, Dad, come in. These are my new friends. Ron meditates; I told him you do too."

When the guys trooped downstairs for a snack, Mr. Mars told me to sit cross-legged on the bed, opposite him, and told me about himself.

"During the War, I fought against Rommel in Africa. We were in the LRDRG, the Long-Range Desert Reconnaissance Group."

"Wow," I said. "What a coincidence, I've just finished reading the Bantam War book, The Phantom Major, about Major David Stirling who founded the SAS Commandos, and the LRDRG took them across the Sahara Desert, penetrating deep behind German-Italian lines, on sabotage missions.

Mr. Mars smiled. "Mostly we lay up along *Jerry's* communication lines. Our vehicles were camouflaged, and we gathered intelligence on enemy troop movements. The trick was getting back in one piece. We had some bloody close calls, lost a few of our mates, but I must say, it was jolly good fun at times!"

Having my full attention, Mr. Mars delved into his meditation practice. "You need a guru's blessing and direction for tangible results, like psychic power and astral projection..." He ran through a brief description of the chakras and kundalini, which I'd already read about, and then sat up straight.

"Now visualize. Imagine that your guru is seated in the lotus position above your head. His white blessings flow down into your body and mixes with the red kundalini rising up from your sex chakra. Focus on your third eye, the spot on your forehead between your eyes, until you see a blinding light. It takes time and patience, so you may as well get started, even though you don't have a qualified guru yet."

It was hard to sit still and focus, but I kept at it, convinced that I'd found a part of my life's mission. The dawning of the Age of Aquarius and a positive social revolution was neigh upon us.

42

THE DEATH OF A FRIEND

When I finished my probation duties, officer Sample glanced at the floor and bathroom sink and nodded his approval. "Looks good, kid. You can go now." That was how my job ended on a normal day, but this was not a normal day.

Three cops leaned over the desk in the station, looking at snapshots, and one of them waved me over. "Kid, come look at this."

"Don't show him that," Sample said. "It'll give him nightmares."

"He needs to see what can happen to careless punks like him." He thumbed through the colorful Polaroid snapshots, one image at a time. I stared at them without comprehending. The images looked like bits of clothing, with what appeared to be smears of red paint scattered around a background of gravel and grass. Maybe it was evidence of littering or vandalism, and they thought I did it or knew who did.

He shuffled to what was unmistakably a clean tennis shoe, the laces neatly tied. It stood upright between the railroad track rails, as if someone's shoe came off in a chase. As I stared at it, I realized that a white sock sprouted from it along with the bloody stump of a severed ankle. I recognized bloody body parts, strips of clothing and flesh scattered along the railroad tracks. Besides the foot, one last picture stuck in my mind, a section of a mangled and headless human torso still clothed in a white tee shirt.

Sample refused to show me the head. He spoke gravely. "This is what a speeding train can do when it smacks into you."

We had to be careful walking along the tracks, sure, but the roads were no safer. Wood Dale still didn't have sidewalks. We had to walk or ride our bikes along a gravel shoulder that erosion sometimes narrowed to a few inches and get honked at by rush hour traffic.

One of the cops gave me the rundown. The speeding train blasted its horn, like it always did at the crossing of Irving Park and Wood Dale Roads, but the boy ducked under the lowered gates, and got hit. It took time and distance for the train to come to a stop, dropping pieces of the boy's body all along the tracks as far as the trestle over Salt Creek.

Sample sighed and shook his head. "The engineer said the kid didn't even look up. Was he playing chicken? What the hell was he thinking? We had to photograph this mess for our investigation before we bagged him up. It made me sick to my stomach."

Officer Sample scrutinized me. "He lived close by, a few years older than you. Maybe you knew him." He didn't tell me his name, and I didn't ask.

"Alright, kid." Sample gave me a nudge. "Scram, you're outta here. Stay out of trouble and keep your nose clean."

I continued down Edgebrook Road to Paul's house, and he hailed me from the yard.

"Ron, did'ja hear? Charlie Diezel bought it."

"Huh?"

"He got hit by a train yesterday. Man, can you believe it?"

Charlie was five years older than me, the oldest brother of Paul's friends, Mike and George, who founded our club of Woods Runners, but he was more on the edge of my social circle and I never really got to know him as an individual. His death was a shock.

Paul raised questions about the circumstances of Charlie's sudden demise. "He had to have heard the train whistle. I can hear it clear across town. Was he playing chicken or was it suicide?" Paul's face was grim. "The last time I saw him, it seemed like he had something on his mind, like he was bummed out about something, but I brushed it off and didn't ask him about it."

Charlie left no note, no indication that he was depressed as far as I knew. He'd been a quiet, unassuming guy, almost twenty years old, with his whole life before him, and maybe that's what scared him.

He was not the last of my friends to be killed in a collision, whether drunk or sober, hit by cars, trains, or driving into trees at full speed. Collisions outranked murder and drug overdoses among my friends in the coming years.

Charlie's brothers were busy comforting their distraught parents. Masses would be celebrated, rosaries recited, saints implored to intercede for his soul, but Paul and I decided Charlie deserved a more heroic send-off. Whether or not he intended to die, he'd crossed the great divide to explore new dimensions, which all of us would do someday.

It seemed fitting that I pour out a libation for his hovering spirit, and toast Charlie's new adventure with as much ostentation as he deserved. With my eyes turned skyward, I shouted into the vastness of the Cosmos. "Death is not the end of us!"

A far too brief obituary in the local paper summed up Charlie's life:

Charles W. Diezel. Born 1947, died Sep. 11, 1967. Son of George and Mercedes Diezel… Struck and killed by an oncoming train near the Wood Dale, Illinois train station. Burial: Saint Joseph Cemetery, River Grove, Cook County, Illinois.

43

RETURN TO STUDY HALL

My sophomore year began. A few girls sat at the long table at the far end of the study hall. Perfect, that's where I'd sit, and I looked forward to flirting with them. Then, *bam!* Someone slammed into me from behind and tore my textbooks from my grip, scattering my assignments across the floor. Spinning around, I saw Sam, a blond greaser, clapping in triumph.

"Ha-ha, dork. I got you, stupid loser! You gonna do something about it? Ha, Schulz is nothing but a wimp."

The bell rang, and he jumped into his seat at the far end of the study hall just as the teacher walked into the room. She was a bespeckled old woman who taught math and brooked no nonsense in study hall. She glared at me, the only student not in a seat. I was still gathering my stuff off the floor.

"When the bell rings, I expect you to be seated," she said. "Do you think this is some kind of a joke? Hurry up, gather your things and sit. There is to be no dilly-dallying here."

This was the second time Sam did this. I tried to shrug it off, but the girls tittered with glee as I plunked down across from them, and I knew they had lost any regard they might have had for me. Word got around fast in high school and if I didn't make that jerk Sam pay for it, I would forever after be branded as a wimp in everyone's mind, even my own. I needed to wipe that contemptuous sneer off his face. It was better to go down fighting than be called a wimp. I couldn't afford to go back to the way things were.

The words in my textbook were blurred. I couldn't focus on even my favorite subjects. I'd have to cream that son of a bitch, and soon. Big John, the tormentor of my freshman year, had dropped out of school to join the Marines and test his mettle in the jungles of Vietnam, but plenty of other bullies took his place. Sam wasn't as huge and muscular as John, but he was still a bigger, stronger, and a more experienced fighter than me, so I'd have to pull a Pearl Harbor attack, nail him hard and fast before he could react.

The stories that Mr. Mars, my friend's dad, told me of sneaking around enemy positions in the Sahara Desert during the War put flesh on the history I read. He had been there, risking his life, doing heroic things, and I took inspiration from him as I planned ways for me to cream that son of a bitch.

The next time I returned to the same room, I carried an extra large bundle of books at my side, and walked toward my seat with a slouched and careless gait, as if I was the perfect victim, but it was only a pretense. Using my peripheral vision, I watched Sam smirking as he elbowed one of his chortling comrades, but I kept my back toward him, so he'd think he snuck up on me. With my senses keyed up like sonar, I listened to him creeping up on me. When I sensed he was close enough, I let him have it.

Wham! I swung my books like a battering ram into his gut. It doubled him over and I turned and grabbed his neck before he could react and slammed him against the table, which came crashing down with us to the floor. His face registered dumb surprise as I wrapped his chin to his knees under my body, like a pretzel, holding onto his thrashing body for all I was worth. We rolled around and slammed into tables and chairs, sweating, swearing, gasping for air, giving it our all.

A crowd formed around us, chanting, "Fight! Fight! Fight!"

My attack worked better than I expected. He tried to punch me from his awkward position, but sliding my elbow around his neck; I grabbed his fists and held on. It took some maneuvering to balance my lighter body on top of his, but I kept him pinned down until he crumpled, helpless.

"Give up, Sam!" I hoped he would, because I couldn't hold him much longer.

"Okay, man," he said, his voice rasping into his chest. "You win. Jeez!"

Although I was unsure if he'd come back at me, I released him. The bell rang just as an overweight, middle-aged teacher ran in screaming from the hall.

"You boys get up right now. I mean it! Everyone clear out of the way!"

Giggling behind their hands, the girls enjoyed the show. Trying to appear nonchalant, I righted the knocked-over table and started to sit down.

"Not so fast, young man," the teacher said. "Both of you boys pick up your books and march yourselves down the hall to the principal's office. Let him deal with this nonsense!"

This wasn't nonsense. It made the most sense to me since I landed in Fenton. I had finally done the right thing. Fighting back was the only way to be respected in the eyes of my peers. Even our teachers, whatever else they told us, fawned on bullies, treating them with more care and caution than the rest of us.

Sam laughed nervously as I walked beside him to the principal's office while keeping a wary eye on him. He stuck out his right hand and clapped my shoulder with his left, as if we'd become pals.

"I really didn't think ya had it in ya, Schulz. You caught me off guard, you know, or you never could have whipped me. Not if I'd kept on my feet, you wouldn't. You're a wrestler, huh? I'm not a wrestler; no, man, I'm a boxer. I let you get too close. See? That was my mistake; I should have never let you, no way." On and on he went as we, erstwhile enemies, walked down the deserted hall and presented ourselves to the school receptionist.

"Take a seat," she said, waving at a line of empty chairs.

Sam sat next to me, rambling on with gusto about past brawls, the epic legends of Fenton, while I wondered at the rapid turn of events, and if he would be so eager to befriend me if I'd lost the battle. To be lauded and befriended by a greaser was a novel experience for me, and I thanked the smiling gods of war for my victory. It had been a near thing, and I'd have to do better next time. I'd been reading about the Samurai code, as well as the Roman and Prussian concepts of military honor, and realized that to forgive was what a man of honor ought to do, but for the moment, I would let him kiss my ass.

The office door opened, and Mr. Whitlow, director of Student Discipline, stepped out. His half inch of salt-and-pepper hair stood straight up in a trim flattop. With a smug smile on his face, he demanded a rundown of what happened and pretended to listen, nodding like a wise sage as Sam gave his self-serving version of events, which, of course, omitted his provocation. Sam made it sound like a bit of roughhousing taken too far, and I nodded along in mute agreement with his version.

Mr. Whitlow fixed me with his steely eyes. "Anything to add, Mr. Schulz?"

"No." I said, preferring to hold my silence and let Sam yak it up.

"Well then, I hope you boys have settled your differences. Are you ready to go back to class and behave yourselves?" He sounded bored and I could almost read his mind.

These fights, and worse, happened every day at Fenton, and to put a lid on unruly students, his administration promoted a stricter dress code than some other schools like Addison Trail. Their more lax dress code allowed too much individual expression, and the school filled up with long-haired hippies, boys walking around with sideburns and their shirttails out. Fenton made every effort to come down hard on nonconformist behavior. Parents wanted him to instill strict discipline in their kids so they could better fit into society.

He sent us on our way with time enough to make it back for the last few minutes of study hall. Halfway there, Sam clapped my shoulder and crowed, "We sure showed him. Didn't we, buddy?"

"Great," I said. It looked like we were pals now, but I remained wary and unsure whether accepting his friendship would make me an accessory to his bullying other students. No, I had standards and would not cross that line.

Back in my seat, I watched the girls giggle and make signs to each other as I meditated on the fickle fortunes of war. There hadn't been any blood, black eyes, or torn shirts in our short tussle. It was a small affair in the scheme of Fenton fights, and yet my status improved and I was making a wider range of friends.

44

THE CHIMES OF FREEDOM

A new dark-haired boy sat at the far end of the long lunch table, gesturing with his hands as he harangued his tablemates. "Fenton is the most fascist high school in the whole Chicago area! I ought to know, man. Before my parents moved to Wood Dale, I attended several other schools. None of them were as bad as this shit hole."

Intrigued, I broke into the conversation. "I couldn't agree with you more. We need to fight back against the establishment." I held out my hand. "I'm Ron Schulz, by the way."

"Ron, I'm Dave Hickey. Glad to meet you." Dave and I became instant friends and conspirators. I let him roar away as he filled me in on the full story of his introduction to Fenton.

"I arrived at Fenton the day before the great blizzard of 1967. Remember that? Shit, I had to take the entrance exam, but I got here late and I'd forgotten the damn room number. My hair was just a little long, Beatle's style. That was acceptable where I'd gone to school before. Somebody warned me that my long hair would have to go, but I thought I'd take care of it after I enrolled."

He stopped to guzzle the rest of his cup of juice and went on. "Unsure where to go, I stood in the hall looking for someone to ask, and along came this fat-fuck of a Phys-Ed teacher. I later learned that he taught Driver's Ed too. Damn, he was angry, the fucker! He didn't even bother to ask me for my pass, but balled me out, with his finger in my face, about how disgusting I looked."

Dave grabbed my arm, fixing me with an intense gaze. "The teacher said, 'how could you ever be allowed to represent the fine students of such a great school as Fenton.' Well Ron, I hadn't even enrolled yet, and I found myself being suspended! Shit, I hadn't even taken my entrance exam yet." His eyes popped wide open in disbelief. "They told me to go home and not return until I cleaned up my 'dirty hair and rebellious dress,' as they called it, and right there I vowed that I would take them down!"

"Cool, Dave," I said and banged my fist on the table in a show of support. "We ought to start an underground newspaper, and see if we can radicalize this complacent student body."

"I hope so, Ron. Bensenville is the most conservative of the working-class towns in Du Page County. Even so, they're snubbed by that filthy rich, fundamentalist, Wheaton, which is the home to Billy Graham's College. We've got to stand up to them, Ron, and put a stop to their highhanded crap."

And so, we started an underground newspaper. Dave introduced me to his friends who joined our project. The somber Dennis Harris lent me books on Tibetan mysticism. Ed "The Poet" Walter scribbled poems and ideas non-stop. Steve Rock was a well-read expert on Native American lore, who, like me, saw their cultures as pivotal to the Age of Aquarius that was dawning all around us, and just maybe, we were those Native Americans reincarnated.

We saw ourselves as wild spirits coming back to reclaim this stolen land and usher in a new era of love and enlightenment. Dave's younger brother Tim earned his place on the team, putting in long hours typing up articles that their supportive mother mimeographed into the finished product. Then there was John Luke.

John was already over eighteen and refused to cut his long hair, something that the administration had never allowed. I suppose his age made him a special case, as well as his situation. Both of his parents had been killed in a car accident. Having no family, he lived alone in the Bensenville flophouse nicknamed the Snake Pit, and worked in the rail yards, saving his money so he could finish high school and get a better job. But as with the rest of us, Fenton's administration insisted that unless he conformed to the dress code and cut his hair, they would kick him out.

John embodied everything the so-called adults in the administration could want. He was an ambitious, self-sufficient guy, paying his own way, and trying to finish his education to get a better job than manual labor. Still, they hounded and threatened him.

He and Dave fought back, calling this a First Amendment issue. Therefore, we made the school dress code the theme of our first issue. It was a novel idea to imagine that underage students had rights, but he was an adult with a draft card. Dave's mother was shocked and came on board to help us. I never mentioned it to my parents. Dave's folks were more understanding than mine.

Dennis wrote a moving piece about the Vietnam War. Dave added a page proposing a Student Union with a constitution that said, among other things, that if the administration got out of hand or didn't give us what we demanded, we would strike. I gave these guys encouragement but didn't manage to get my far-flung ideas condensed into a coherent message on paper.

We called our newspaper The Chimes of Freedom, with a nod to the Simon and Garfunkel song and were off and running as Fenton's first and only underground newspaper in the nineteen sixties. Dissent was verboten at Fenton, even though Civil Rights and the Vietnam War had only been addressed by Dennis' imaginative story, but even that was too much. The administration shut us down after only two issues that we passed out, for free, in the halls between classes.

Dave, Tim, and I took weekend trips to explore Chicago, where we talked to local and well-traveled hippies in Old Town and befriended Iranian members of the Baha'i faith who believed that all religions came from a common source. When the snows fell, we went winter camping on the weekend in Busse Woods, north of Wood Dale, just to toughen ourselves up.

These were my radical hippie friends, but I stayed close to the greasers I'd befriended, too. There was no good reason for us to limit ourselves to a narrow circle. The stranger, I believed, was the friend we hadn't met, although we did have to be wary of some.

We all listened to rock and roll and I discovered a band I hadn't heard before named Country Joe and the Fish. They came out with a new song titled *I Feel Like I'm fixin' to Die Rag*. Its darkly comic lyrics about the Vietnam War spoke to me, especially the next-to-last verse that parodied breakfast cereal ads. It went: "Be the first one on your block, to have your boy come home in a box."

It was no joke. I watched the news and read articles about the growing body count. More and more American boys were coming home in boxes, but it bothered me that no one seemed to care about all the Vietnamese boys and girls who didn't even get boxes after being incinerated by napalm. Maybe we weren't the good guys in this war.

45

SEPTEMBER 1968: BIG JOHN RETURNS

Another school year began, and I was a junior. Don, one of my new greaser pals, pulled up into my driveway, got out of the car and faced me with a furrowed brow. "Hey, Ron, did you hear? Big John is back from Vietnam."

I didn't know what to say at first. John had made my freshman year a living hell before I ran away to New Orleans. He dropped out of high school soon after to join the Marines when his parents signed for him. By some bizarre twists of fate, including the fight with Sam and hanging out with some new friends of Paul and Mark Ladendorf, I found myself befriended by a few greasers, including Don, to whom Big Bad John was a hero. But I wondered why Don looked so concerned.

He stared at me for a moment without a word, and then he said, "John is dead. He was killed in action in Vietnam."

That took me by surprise. "What the fuck, man? Are you sure?"

My emotions tumbled around, alternating between relief and the compassion my growing Buddhist faith required me to feel for all living beings, even enemies. I couldn't help thinking that the Viet Cong did me a favor, but I restrained my feelings out of diplomatic courtesy.

Jake, another greaser with his hair slicked back, stepped out of the passenger side of the car and grabbed my shoulder. "It's true, Ron. His body came home in a closed casket; he must have gotten blown to smithereens."

"Yeah," Don said, nodding in agreement. "They probably just picked up the pieces off the battlefield and tossed 'em in a body bag. For all we know, they could've grabbed some of the wrong soldier's parts too and put 'em in the casket."

"Yeah, man," Jake said. "Wouldn't it be crazy if they accidentally included pieces of a dead gook?"

That would be a hell of a cosmic joke, or karmic justice, but I didn't laugh, although I wondered if John had bullied the Vietnamese as he had me. How bizarre it was that I'd wound up hanging out with some of his friends, but I wanted to believe in human potential. No one, including that son of a bitch, could be all bad, or all good.

Jake waved me to the car. "Come with us to the funeral."

"Okay, sure," I said, feeling that the Wheel of Karma had spun me off into a strange twilight zone.

We drove to Geil's Funeral Home in Bensenville. I hung in the background, feeling out of place among John's friends and family, most of whom were strangers, except for a few who had been downright hostile to me in the past. They didn't seem to recognize me, and I didn't want to yak with them about ancient history, anyway.

That hellish time seemed so long ago, but only a single year had passed, a year in which so much happened that it made my head spin. Once upon a time I had been a freshman and a loser and although I was beginning to feel a little more confident, I was still lost. But I was alive and Big John was dead.

Our destiny pulls us in mysterious ways, and I was curious. Why, I wondered, did John hate me so much? Surrounded by strangers, I listened in as they expressed grief and shared memories of him. Their stories surprised me; John had a side I never imagined.

"John was such a great guy," a skinny greaser, a little older than me, said. "At my first Fenton dance in my sophomore year, six bad asses jumped me. John stepped in to even the odds. He was more than a match for all of them put together and those guys never bothered me again."

His friend wiped away a tear. "Yeah, John was a friend of mine, too. I remember him with a big smile on his face. He'd walk up and just say 'Hey man.' It made everything better somehow."

"Yeah," an older man standing nearby said. "John was a pretty good boy. His name, John Wayne, fit him. He wanted to be a Marine in the worst way, ever since he could talk."

He pulled out a newspaper. "It says he was killed on September fourteenth, and he'd only been in Vietnam since June. That's less than three months. He must have been out on a patrol when he got blown up."

Someone grabbed the paper. "Look at this. John was the fifth boy from the neighborhood to die in Vietnam this year. Well, sure, he knew that he would get sent there when he signed up. He told me he had a premonition that he'd never come back alive, and he said that he didn't fit into ordinary life anyway, that there was nothing for him to look forward to around here. Can you believe that?"

Listening in, I realized that John had been a lost soul too, maybe as lost as me. Neither of us fit in to the society we grew up in. He never actually laid a hand on me; left that to his companions, but his words, filled with so much malice and contempt, were poisonous. Like magical incantations, curses, or prayers, words carry the emotional power to hurt or heal.

They buried John in Mount Emblem Cemetery in Elmhurst, and he later got his name inscribed on the wall of the slain in Washington, DC.

The next year would be 1969. I'd turn seventeen, and insist on quitting school legally, so my parents wouldn't send the storm troopers after me when I left to explore the world. A whole new chapter of my life would begin. I'd take off for the fresh air of the New Mexico and Colorado Rockies to join hippie communes and an open marriage. My journey to the wild side hadn't ended. It had only just begun.

RONALD SCHULZ

 RONALD SCHULZ was born in the nineteen-fifties in Chicago. He dropped out to explore the Sixties radical counterculture before hitchhiking across Europe and Africa on a roundabout Buddhist pilgrimage to Nepal. Now a semi-retired hobo, and a new author writing his honest history of those tumultuous times, he hopes to honor the memory of departed friends before he too vanishes from this planet. He has taken advanced writing classes at the University of Washington and Hugo House. Ronald is a father of two, grandfather of three, who believes in living life to the fullest, regardless of circumstances.

ALSO BY RONALD SCHULZ

Chicago Rage

Home at the Edge

Party at the End of the Rainbow

If you enjoyed this work, please leave a rating on Goodreads and the platform where you purchased it. Your feedback helps the author and encourages them to write more works for your enjoyment.